Audiovisual Production

Adrian Vance

AMPHOTO
American Photographic Book Publishing Co.
New York

All photographs by the author.

Copyright © 1979 by Adrian Vance. All rights re-
served. No part of this book may be reproduced in any
form whatsoever without written permission from the
publisher. Published in New York, New York by American Photographic Book Publishing Co., Inc.

Library of Congress Cataloging in Publication Data

Vance, Adrian.
  Audiovisual production.

  Includes index.
  1. Photography, Commercial. 2. Audio-visual
materials. I. Title.
TR690.V36   778   79-12761

ISBN 0-8174-2480-6 (hardbound)

Manufactured in the United States of America

Table of Contents

Introduction

Audiovisual production is a business, a creative enterprise, and a logistic system. To be successful in this field it is necessary to understand many skills. It is not necessary to master all of them because they are usually available at reasonable prices. The small producer may have to master many of the specialities covered in this book, but even the biggest producer should understand them nearly as well. It does not matter whether you are making a lecture slide show, a filmstrip, a motion picture, or videotape. The process is the same. While the major budget decisions can be made very quickly in a small slide show, they may take longer in a motion picture. But the decisions still come down to "How much?" and "From where?"

Every step of the audiovisual production process has been analyzed in this way; the conclusions are outlined on these pages. This work best applies to the filmstrip and multi-image fields, as these are the areas of our greatest experience. However, the principles are the same throughout the field. The theory of our approach has been that there is a basic principle underlying every skill, whether it be writing, photography, or sound. In writing, the objective and the outline are keys to success; in photography, an understanding of light is the secret to success; and in working with sound, knowing the principles of music is the answer. You will find all of these things in this book, and we have tried to explain them with utter clarity.

1

Creating A Project

THE IMPETUS

The creation of an audiovisual project does not have to be a revelatory experience. There are too many problems in education, business, industry, recreation, and daily living for you to have to wait for a bolt of lightning from Heaven to tell you what to do. In most cases the audiovisual creative process fulfills a need. So well does this need outline the task, that in most cases there is no need to wait for a starting impulse. In this field you are in large measure converting materials from the printed page to the screen, or you are bringing together information, the pictures and sounds of things, to be assembled in a new and different way. This expands the problem to one of making choices.

THE CHOICES

There are now so many choices of media, ranging from a cassette tape to a dramatic motion picture, with every kind of slide show, filmstrip, motion picture, and video program in between, that you are wise to keep the choice of medium open as long as possible during your initial planning phase. In one recent case we were asked to do a simple slide show for a major record production-distribution company. The president of the firm wanted something he could take to the NARM (National Association of Record Merchandisers) convention, show in his hotel suite, and give a running talk. During the initial discussions we changed the plan to that of making a filmstrip, then a three-projector dissolve show with edited music on tape, and finally, a six-projector fully automated show run by an AVL Show Pro V.

The show was such a success that the client came back to us for three major revisions, took the show from Hawaii to New York and Canada, and is now talking about something spectacular for the next convention/meeting season. This client did not come to us with a silver shovel filled with money to spend on this project. Here again, as always, was another hard-headed businessman who didn't get rich being foolish; he had a project and was ultimately willing to spend if he could get a big bang for his buck. You can never find out how much your potential client is willing to spend at the beginning. What he spends is part of his behavior pattern. If he is a plunger he will spend freely for an audiovisual project, as he will for anything else.

In terms of style there are many choices within all media. The importance of capable writing cannot be overestimated. It is absolutely crucial to any project to have a clear objective, a target audience, coherent ideas, and appropriate language. The writing problem will be dealt with very directly in a later chapter, but at this point it can be said that the most important starting point is the objective. The easiest shows to do are those with a single objective, and the toughest ones are those with no objective or too many objectives. Audiovisual shows have become so popular that many companies have them made with no thought of an objective other than some kind of splash at a convention, a distributor meeting, or a sales meeting. It should be very apparent initially that the planners of the show have a clear idea of how they are going to use it. Will the president of the company stand up and speak immediately after the presentation? Or, will he introduce it? A few simple questions of this kind will very much help you to make style choices.

Planning sessions with management people should be structured so you, as the producer, spend your initial hours listening to what is wanted, the middle sessions telling them what is possible, and the final stage deciding what will be done. The time involved in these planning sessions will seldom exceed more than two or three hours, and each meeting should be scheduled for 30 minutes or one hour. Some companies like marathon meetings, but few can plan them effectively. From our own observations it seems that meetings that go beyond one hour become counterproductive. In any event, your final meeting, in which the show will be pretty well defined, should take no more than one hour. If this meeting begins to stretch, or if the entire process takes more than one week, the project is going to be troublesome because indecision or a communication problem has evolved.

Every show or audiovisual project will have one vexing problem, and in most cases it will happen, or be defined, at the beginning. If the management people cannot make up their minds as to what they want, but *must* have a show, you will have to invent an acceptable objective and sell it to them. If they cannot make up their minds and *may not* have a show, i.e. there is no deadline, convention, meeting, or whatever, then you will have to wait them out or look for another project. It is far easier to work for an outfit that is run by a tyrant than one that is managed by a committee. In the former situation, the power is at the top, and you can usually find out what is on the boss's mind by simply listening; most of what other people say is unimportant. Unfortunately, the age of the magnate seems to have passed, and most companies are run by groups of people pulling in several different directions. Often these are just the companies that come to an audiovisual producer because they are looking for a miracle that will pull their forces together and make a single-minded corporation out of the committee. You just may be the one who can do it.

THE PROCESS

The following are several example cases of how audiovisual projects happened, and from these you may see how the creative process works in this field.

A number of years ago I was wrapping up an educational filmstrip project for a large company, and the final stage of the process involved the making of the sound tracks. I had spent considerable time in the recording studio and developed a good working relationship with the owner. At that time his business was new, and he was energetic and casting about for ways to expand his business. On my last day there he asked me into his office and discussed the possibility of our getting together on a project. I would supply the idea, script, and direction, and he and his prople would take care of the technical and manufacturing problems for a cassette recording. It sounded very good to me. The cassette business was really starting to happen, and I surveyed the market and decided there was an opportunity for a cassette entitled "Want To Stop Smoking?" He bought the idea, and we were soon in business together on this one project. This is a pleasant and convenient way to do business. You are totally in control of the situation. The responsibilities are defined, and there are no grinding inefficiencies in the process. But, the situation needs one thing that did not happen in this case: success in the marketplace. I can now tell you how many people don't want a recording on how to stop smoking.

An earlier occurrence, and one much more successful in terms of outcome, was my first audiovisual project produced while I was in my first year of teaching. In my three sections of high-school biology, there was a microscrope for each student, and virtually the first activity was to teach the students how to use the instruments. I discovered that there was no combination of words, number of repetitions, blackboard illustrations, or demonstrations from my table at the front of the room that would explain the microscope to these young people in a way that would render them capable of using it. Two or three students seemed to figure it out, but all the rest needed a one-to-one presentation. This was just unacceptable to me—a vexing challenge at the base of my course. There had to be a solution.

I decided that the difficulty was that the students couldn't really *see* what it was I was talking about. So, I photographed a sequence of pictures showing how to do everything and how the specimen looked through the eyepiece when the image was out of focus, almost in focus, and in focus. In addition, through the microscope I photographed the letter *e* from a newspaper, as well as biological specimens. What I had forgotten after all my years of familiarity with this equipment is that things don't look like the students' expectations. This slide sequence, which initially had no more than 20 frames, turned the situation about completely, and whereas only one or two students would understand the microscope the first time around without the slide sequence, only one or two would *not* understand it after seeing the slides. This was a powerful lesson for me in 1960, and one that I will never forget.

I took the show to The Society For Visual Education in Chicago in March 1960. The management people there were very impressed by it, but they would not attempt to sell one filmstrip. In order for them to take it, I would have to do three or four more slide shows to be converted to filmstrips. Now my creative urge had to come from another direction because the objective in this case simply was to fill the package. Nonetheless, I did manage to keep my original idealism intact, as none of the basic preparation techniques had been photographed for a filmstrip that would be projected in a way that every student in the class could see it. None of us then realized how important this work would soon be because biology classes were still small, usually 20 students or less. But in the '60s classes grew to 30 or 40 students per class, far too many to gather around the teacher's desk to see a demonstration.

To say that this filmstrip series was a success would be to understate the case in the extreme. To date nearly half of the high schools in the country have purchased it, and after 18 years on the market it is still selling almost as well as it did in its second and third years, the normal peak for a filmstrip. This occurred in spite of the fact that this filmstrip has no sound track and none of the high production value put into new filmstrips. It simply works, and that is what is needed by the schools.

Sales and training shows have to work too, and an excellent case in point is a filmstrip we made a few years ago for a barter-trade corporation. They had previously paid for the production of two motion pictures and another filmstrip all designed to explain the workings of their barter-trade system. The system is complicated by the fact that the trading is done in part cash and part trade credits. The members are classified according to their cost of doing business, where the basic idea is that the cash portion will repay their material or inventory cost, and their profit is taken in trade credits. The earlier shows had muddied the water with a lot of promotion about the benefits of the system without really explaining it. That is not the way to sell something like this to an audience of businessmen. Therefore, in my first script the total objective was to explain the system with a minimum of glitter. This would have been a seven- or eight-minute show.

The management of the barter-trade organization liked the script but wanted to add a lot of material to it. Some of it was legal information, some was bragging of past accomplishments, and finally, some was their grand plan for the future. I didn't want any of this in the show, but the client was paying for it. The final show was 18½ minutes long, and while everyone agreed that it was good, everyone also admitted that it was too long. This resulted in a second show that was trimmed down to eight minutes with about one minute of hard sell tagging it. I could not complain about getting two prices for one show, but it is more fun to do it right the first time.

When making industrial and sales training shows you have to be ready to let the client do it his way the first time and let him discover the leaner, better presentation in the process. At today's prices you don't see too many unknowledgeable people trying to buy audiovisual shows. Corporation people still seem to have to learn the basic lessons about audiovisual production before they are capable of intitiating an audiovisual show. We are finding that the educated clients, those with some experience in this field, are more often giving us the assignment and the cooperation of their people and then letting us alone. We will soon be doing two more filmstrips for the barter-trade organization, and we will have one meeting with the president of the firm and no contact with the legal department by his edict. He will see the final script once, we will do it, and that's it. This kind of working relationship is something that has to be developed over a period of time.

The home market is a market that has really not been available to audiovisual producers, and we have only had fleeting experience with it, essentially through producing television commercials. Still, this is not really producing for the home market as much as it is inflicting a corporation on this market. The home market will happen for the small audiovisual producer when video tape and the video disc become common in the home. This is just a matter of time and the setting up of a distribution system.

The present system of broadcast television is a system that can do nothing better than produce the same kind of product it has made for the 30 years it has existed in this country. The severe demand of producing even a 30-minute weekly show means that all functions have to be reduced to a formula, and anything experienced too often will become tiresome. Video tape and the video disc can break the present system's stranglehold on what we see and give us some choices. It is only this kind of competition that also will increase the quality of what is available. Most television programs now have no meaning and little entertainment value. In the future all television programs will have to have meaning and entertainment value, or people will do something else.

We are on the brink of an educational revolution in this country, if not in the entire western culture. When the general public learns that the difference between the person who has a life with meaning and the one who does not is information, the educational revolution will happen. If even a small fraction of the general public suddenly acquired this idea, the shelves of all the public libraries would become empty overnight. The printing presses and paper mills of this world cannot supply the potential demand for information when the general public wants it. The only solution is electronic production of information, and the only people who come anywhere near meeting the demand are the audiovisual producers. We expand the information, its potential, and its use.

The longer you are in this business the more impressed you will be with the ability of its products to teach, sell, and change people. If the invention of the printed page has given us the civilization in which we live, audiovisual systems will perfect it. Most of our citizens really do not read; they leave that task to others, not realizing that in so doing they lose control. Information is now the most important resource we have, and because audiovisual systems can produce information in a consumable form with little viewer effort, there will be no escape from information in the audiovisual era.

2

Selling A Project

Selling is an activity that is always part of audiovisual production. A well-established producer may not appear to be making a regular effort of selling, but his body of work is doing it for him. If his work is not visible and functioning, if the flow of it is interrupted, or if there are large personnel changes in his client's management, he will have to drum the territory in the same fashion as the rank beginner.

Selling audiovisual programs should really be a difficult thing because the fact of the matter is that you are trying to promote something that does not exist. The sale is made in two ways: (a) by example and (b) in the client's ability to fantasize the product that will result in his case. This latter, less visible mechanism is the most important quantity in the selling equation. I would rather go in and show a potential client a blank screen and give him a glowing talk about how great his product will look on it than show him something inappropriate or poorly done. We actually did this in the case of a very special client problem in the entertainment industry, and the company bought it. In all fairness, people in "show-biz" have more imagination than most other businessmen, but the element of projection on the part of the client is important in all audiovisual selling.

In general, you are dealing with five distinct markets in audiovisual production. There are smaller sub-markets within these categories, but each of these five markets has a distinct set of characteristics, traditions, and practices such that each has to be approached and dealt with in a unique manner. It is important for you to remember that you are coming from the audiovisual business into these fields, and you too have special requirements. If your client is new to the audiovisual field, he will require some education, and this is your responsibility. The following are definitions of these five markets.

INDUSTRIAL TRAINING

This is probably the most straightforward market to sell to because you must show this type of client a sample of your work in the form of a finished show, (an automatic slide show or filmstrip show), and he will usually decide rather quickly. If you want to be in this business, you may have to make a sample program showing some manufacturing process, repair operation, or mechanical explanation. In making the sample you also may be able to make your first deal, as the example can show a service that could logically be needed by a potential client. As long as you are going to have to do a sample anyway, why not do one that could net some future business? It has been our experience that once you plant the audiovisual seed in a corporation it only grows.

A very nice feature of this business is that all of the selling, the planning meetings, and final screenings take place in the client's office. You can have the worst barn of a production studio and never be embarrassed about it because the client does not see it. If you are doing industrial training shows, much, if not all, of the photography takes place at the client's facility, and this also reduces your studio requirements. A minimum studio should include a copy stand for art up to 11" × 14", and preferably bigger, a flat wall 3 × 6 m (10' × 20') with 6 m (20 ft) of flat, level floor in front of it, and an office and meeting room with light boxes for editing. The flat wall in the studio section can be used for a projection screen; most of the time this wall will be white, but you should be ready to paint it any color needed. Paint works much better than seamless paper in photography, costs less, and requires no storage, but does take more time to handle.

If you decide to make a sample show for potential clients, you can use any music, sound effect, and photography in existence to demonstrate what you can do with these elements. You can legally use anything up to the point of being paid for it under the "reasonable use" provisions of the copyright law. This can give you a very punchy show, but it generates two problems down the line. First, your client may go into shock when he finds out how much this kind of production can cost in terms of getting releases and renting the images. And second, it is far better to show as many of *your* talents as possible. The more of *your* work the client will buy, the more you net on the project. We have observed that clients in the industrial field, visually sophisticated or not, usually like things that are fairly simple and straight to the point. They don't care whether or not you are the greatest producer in the world. They have a problem and hope you have a solution.

In the industrial training field price is very important in the deal. Everything is done by bid, and these people will usually go to considerable length to save a few hundred dollars. The larger industrial firms are called on regularly by audiovisual producers, and they keep extensive files on potential sources and their prices. At the point where their annual audiovisual expenditure reaches two or three salaries in the field, these clients will begin to look into setting up their own audiovisual unit.

It is very difficult to go back to this type of client and ask for more money. The only way you can raise the price downstream is in the case in which the client has asked for revisions or additions to a show previously contracted and in production. When this happens be sure to memo the executive in charge of the project telling him that the original price is no longer operative. You may or may not want to give an estimate of how much more will have to be added. I prefer to let it ride until the end of the cycle. It is only then that you can be sure what your additional costs and time requirements have been.

Industrial clients usually have their own version of the English language. They prefer engineering-type terminology, speaking of thousands in terms of "K," and using words like "operative" and "deploy." It is very important when working with these people to adopt their language. It results in better communication and identification. Don't be afraid to ask what they mean by some strange-sounding term. Everyone loves to be an expert, and this is the only way you can learn something that you need to know.

SALES

Sales clients are a little easier for most producers to work with than industrial clients. They are less picky about the product, but do insist on a faster pace and some "hype." It is usually fairly easy to satisfy their desires by simply having a lot of flashing images, furious sound effects, and a rich, soothing voice presenting the product or service. The television commercial is the standard of taste in the sales slide show or filmstrip business, but not the super-slick type with a famous female riding a stallion through a misty meadow for a makeup manufacturer. These people seem to like the beer, pretzel, and new car commericals that I can only call "super-tacky." They want to see their product in the most outrageous places being used by a female model, if that makes any kind of sense at all. If pressed, you can shoot one of these shows in a day, but be sure to hire a professional model. They are really worth the money because they are trained for this type of work.

Sales people are fairly loose about prices, and if you run over budget, it is fair to inform them and negotiate an additional fee. There should be some logical reason for the additional cost, and it should not be a surprise when they are hit with it. In some cases it can be due to extended travel, time, and a script revision after production was under way. Script revision is usually caused by the corporation owner who gets a brainstorm after you're rolling. This kind of thing used to irritate me, but I learned after it became a regular occurrence that it meant that the boss was getting interested in the project. There is nothing worse than being ignored in this business, and more often than not the boss actually has a good idea. This occurrence has turned out well for us more often than not, as it gives you a chance to repair earlier errors and charge the client for the cost instead of having to absorb it yourself.

CONVENTIONS AND MEETINGS

This is a very special business that can be totally consuming, and most of the companies that do this work do little else. Most of these shows are now done with multi-projector systems using the AVL Show Pro or Eagle computerized systems or the Spindler-Sauppe Director 24 outfit of a similar type. If you have been doing slide show or filmstrip work for an industrial client, he may ask you to produce this kind of show for his next convention or meeting. This is about the only way a small audiovisual producer happens into this business. Most of the companies that are now in this field have made major investments in equipment and production facilities, and they actively go after this business. You can hire one of these companies to actually produce a show for your client in which you act as the writer-director, perhaps supplying some of the visual material. However, you will find that these systems are so unique that little photography will work with them unless it has been designed especially for them. Much more about this work will be explained in a later chapter, but the essence of the situation is that you can tell your client you can do the show, but it will require your working with a firm that specializes in this type of business.

If you are going to sell this type of show, a ball-park price will have to be about $1200 to $1500 per minute of program if your client wants a state-of-the-art production. If he wants a three-projector dissolve show (nice, but no big splash), and you generally will be working with existing photography, flat art, and other art that he supplies, you may cut the price to $400 to $500 per final minute. Few clients will ask for this type of show until they are confident in the ability of the producer to pull it off and are ready to spend some big money to make the convention or meeting a success. All contracts and business arrangements for these shows must have a 10 percent contingency clause, and you should prepare your client for a somewhat open-ended situation. As liberally as we have budgeted these kinds of shows, we have always gone over and always have had to ask for more money at the end. However, we have been careful, in all but one case, to make the client aware of the problems and additional costs as they occur.

From the outset, selling this kind of show is complicated by the fact that you cannot take the thing into the potential client's office and show it to him. The best choice is to have the client, or some committee of management people, come to a place where your last show can be seen, and let the system sell itself. A really hot multi-image show with a hot sound track is a very special experience. It is different from a motion picture, and the huge potential is immediately apparent. A few of the producers of this type of production have developed automated slide/tape shows that are sufficiently portable to be shown in an office and that show still pictures of some of their prior productions as seen by the audiences. This works fairly well in getting the corporation's management people to come to your facility to see what you have, but it will never sell a deal on its own. For this reason I think that most of these kinds of gimmicks designed to sell multi-image productions are just a waste of time and money.

ENTERTAINMENT

Most selling in entertainment is done by connection and contact. The entertainment industry is one of the most incestuous, inbred, and frustrating businesses in the economy. If you want to be an audiovisual producer in the entertainment industry, the only way to go about it is to find someone in the business needing your creative services and join with him in some way. The best way to go about this, and the only way to limit your liabilities, is to form a corporation. In spite of the several books on this subject, I believe that the best way to go about this is through a lawyer or a corporation of lawyers. Entertainment attorneys are a special breed within the law, and if your partner to be has such a connection, he is the man to set up the corporation.

A corporation of this kind does not have to exist forever. The history of most small production companies shows that they function pretty well for the first couple of years and either get very strong or begin to fade in their third year. Sometimes internal frictions grind away at the company in the second year, but the more usual pattern is that one or more of the partners do not make the full commitment to the enterprise that is needed to make it work. Production companies are probably the most hazardous corporations to make work. Energies are high and tempers can be very short when it looks like the show is going to go down in flames. There quite literally will be times when one of the partners will have to carry an especially heavy load and feel rather alone and taken advantage of by the others. These are the crucial moments in the experience. You just have to grit your teeth and muddle through, promising yourself that you will recognize the situation when the others have to go with the ball and you sit on the sidelines.

The highest point that you can reach in this type of business comes when the show is finished and it works and comes off. You get paid promptly and well, and another job falls to you immediately. The worst experience is that of having a show that just will not come together, does not come off to your expectations, the client is slow to pay, and you discover that you have spent more than you were paid in trying to get it off the ground. You feel absolutely worthless when this happens, and you start admiring people who have regular jobs with salaries, fringe benefits, and a retirement plan. These things happen to all production companies, and sometimes there is no explanation. Being in "show-biz" is rather like riding a pogo stick on a ship at sea; you're never quite sure where you're going to come down.

Price is not a very important consideration in the entertainment business. Most of the production companies are used to spending large quantities of money, but they do expect value for it. The situation is such that you don't have to restrict your expenses on anything, and the basic economics are more like that of building an ocean liner rather than a small boat. There is simply more profit in the big project. The one thing you cannot do to an entertainment client is give him short measure. Once detected, any cheating on a job is tantamount to suicide in the entertainment business. If you go over budget, and have the figures to prove it, there will be little trouble collecting from an entertainment client if the show has come off, gotten good reviews, and pulled a full audience. Entertainment people are used to this kind of thing, and in our experience every show of this kind has had a final budget double the original bid.

At the beginning, entertainment clients will generally try to be rather conservative with the audiovisual budget. As the show begins to form, they will begin to get nervous about everything but the audiovisual components.

In part this is due to too much faith in anything automated and a raising of their own awareness of the effectiveness of media. When these clients see the materials projected, they usually get quite excited about it. They will first ask for small changes and will usually try to overlook the matter of price, thinking, for their own convenience, that this is just part of the normal production situation. At this moment you have to announce that changes make the original budget price invalid—a crisis and hush-producing moment in communication—but that it will only cost such and such. The ice must be cracked at some point, and the very first moment it can happen is the best. If these people ever get the idea that you are going to cut and patch things together for nothing, you'll be doing it up to the moment the show runs, and you will be dead broke at that point.

In addition, the clients will definitely add more to the show in terms of actual material or number of showings. It is for this reason that the production of the material and the showing of it should have two separate budgets. Any time you can reduce the total price of a package in any way, i.e. with two or more fractions, the show will be easier to sell. There is no dishonesty in doing it this way. Anyone with a pencil can add, but they rarely do it in these situations, and it is the best way for you to gain some latitude in doing what you want to do for the show.

Most small audiovisual producers will have to deal with rental houses for the show equipment and hire technical staff to get the production on the screen. The technical staff will consume a major portion of the budget, and it is one cost better left visible to the client because it will give him some important choices. We are fast coming to the day when entertainment clients will want to buy their own projection equipment and hire technicians to run it simply because it will be cheaper than renting the equipment. The rental houses have a standard fee structure of five percent of the equipment price per day rental, and three days equal one week. All setting-up, running, and tearing-down work is done at a high price per hour, but these people are usually fairly quick and efficient. You don't have to be much of a mathematician to see that there is an immense potential in the equipment business, and your client may want to buy the equipment, use it for the show, and sell it afterwards.

EDUCATION

The school market is by far the largest audiovisual market of all, but it is diffused and spread throughout the country. The large educational film and filmstrip distributors, who much prefer to be called producers, like to think of the educational marketplace as a monolith. This would be convenient for their production, selling, and management efforts, but it just isn't true. The educational marketplace is fractured into hundreds of little segments, each with different needs, and no single product line will satisfy any major part of it. It is axiomatic that no educational motion picture or filmstrip series will ever sell more than 1000 prints or sets in a single year. This rule has been broken on only a few occasions; thus we think it is a reasonable top figure. Generally, the largest distributors will sell 300 to 500 copies of a good-selling film or filmstrip set, and the smaller distributors will sell 100 to 300. These are the sales figures in a marketplace where the potential includes 30,000 secondary schools and two to three times as many elementary schools, although the elementary schools probably represent a market equal to that of the secondary schools because many of them are joined, and they are not yet the audiovisual users that the secondary schools have become. If at best the sales effort can hit three percent of the potential, and more normally one percent of the potential, the market has not been properly defined or is not definable. After nearly 60 years of development in the educational audiovisual market, it certainly seems that the market must not be definable.

Still, when you try to sell a project to an educational film or filmstrip company, you have to approach the problem with a market prototype in mind. The managements of these companies make films and filmstrips for a particular type of school with a certain kind of administrator, teacher, and student population set in a community of the type seen on television shows. The fact of the matter is that you can make almost anything you want to for the educational marketplace, and some schools will buy it. But the question has become, "Will the distributors buy it?" The next chapter presents the alternative to dealing with the large distributors, i.e. forming your own distribution company. However, that is an enterprise on a large scale, even if you want to do it in a small way.

Profit in educational films and filmstrips is a long-haul proposition. A typical film or filmstrip project will take two years to pay back its costs because it takes one full year to get sales rolling. Most small producers who make this type of product will do it on the basis of selling it outright on some kind of advance-royalty agreement. Generally, the distributors will advance enough money to make the film or filmstrip set and will negotiate a royalty ranging from 5 to 15 percent, depending on whether or not the royalty is to pay back the advance. There are all kinds of deals in this business, and the quality of the contract, in terms of yield to the producer, depends to a large extent on track record. For the beginner, the person who needs the best contract, such deals are seldom available. The real profit in educational films and filmstrips lies in the royalties, which can run from 12 to 20 years. The money comes in a little each quarter or semi-annually, you pay little tax on it, as there is never that much money at any one time, and it tends to contribute to a stable life style in a business in which that is hard to achieve.

The primary selling tool of educational films and filmstrips is the *treatment*—a feasibility exercise or sometimes a study, which should include a sample script to show the style and producibility of your writing or the writer's writing. In some cases in which you are established, the treatment can be reduced to a telephone call or a letter and a script. The script is the strongest part of the package because this is the closest thing to the product until it is actually made. Educational films and filmstrips have grown into some rather grand projects, and it has been a major failing of many of the would-be writers of material to get carried away with ideas that cannot be produced. It is unfortunate that so many executives in the educational film companies don't understand production well enough to anticipate problems and have to send scripts to readers and various experts. The process of authentication can take many months, typically one year from concept to contract, and the waiting can be difficult.

Authenticity is the big yardstick in educational materials, and it is the most difficult one by which a product can be measured. Experts always feel that they have to say something or the distributor won't think them worthwhile. The hazard in the process is that the ambitious expert may nitpick the project to death. In the most bizarre cases I've had such people prepare 50-page critiques for 10-page scripts, and most of what they said was either nonsense or invention resulting from the fact that they didn't understand the script. Some of these problems have been the result of my own failing to really explain what was happening visually and from the general difficulty in reading scenario format. Few people expert in a field can read scenario format prepared for their own subject matter; it is just too foreign a way of seeing their ideas expressed. The educational field can be the most maddening field to work in, especially if you know something. The producer without academic credentials and experience will not, in all likelihood, be able to work in educational films and filmstrips because the budgets are so small. And the producer who does have such credentials will find a lot of frustration in the process.

3

The Economics of Audiovisual Production

Economics is a near-science, exploring its facts and figures with the mathematical sciences. But economics is written on the water of the river of time—nothing is ever the same, and true sciences require repeatability. Nonetheless, you should try to understand the audiovisual business in economic terms. Certain facts appear to operate in regular ways such that a few rules can be made, but these rules should not be adhered to too rigidly.

CASH FLOW WAVES

The basic economic difficulty in the audiovisual business is that money comes and goes in chunks, and often there are long dry spells between the good times. This requires a reserve or a bank that will lend you money, usually in the form of a loan secured by property or equipment.

If you are starting a production business dealing with industrial, training, sales, and entertainment clients, it is necessary to have a six-month reserve. This can be a combination of cash, credit, and borrowing potential, but it means having enough resources of all kinds to keep the show together for half a year. Some of this time can be bought by reducing overhead to the bone, buying much of what you need from other service suppliers. However, this practice can cut into the profit substantially when you are doing well. The best example is the slide duplicate. Slide duplicates are very easy to make, consume a nickel's worth of materials, but cost 25 to 75 cents from the commercial duplicators. You can set up a slide duplicating system for a few hundred dollars and make back the price in one small job charging only the going rate. In this case the investment is worth it.

Film processing is an example on the opposite side of the coin. Several of the smaller audiovisual producers whom I know have invested in color film processing equipment in part because they felt they could reduce the cost, but in general they were seeking convenience. You really have to be handling an immense amount of film to make one of these machines economically worthwhile, but it is possible to set up a small hand processing system for that occasional roll you *must* see now or process when the lab is closed. Also, if you are a regular customer and get to know the people at your lab, you will be amazed how accommodating they can be. They too are looking at an expensive piece of equipment that really only works well for them when it is functioning all the time.

Most small producers were freelance writer-photographers for some time before they became full-fledged producers, taking full responsibility for the show rather than the pictures or scripts alone. This is the best kind of training, as it puts you in touch with the potential clients and permits you to move fast when you decide to make your move. The one great caution that you must observe in this business is that of not stealing another producer's client or clients if you have been working on staff and not freelancing. If you do steal another producer's client, it will often result in a lawsuit, and defending one of these can ruin you before you get a chance to begin. If you have been working on another producer's staff and want to set up your own shop, about all you can do is quit, open your place of business down the street, pray for business, and try to develop business in places other than those in which your former boss is functioning. If his clients are happy with his service, there is almost no way to get them away from him, and to attempt to do so would be a breach of ethics.

The educational marketplace is a difficult one with which to deal and one that requires one to two years of funding if you intend to be an educational film or filmstrip producer exclusively. This is because most of the educational films and filmstrips produced in recent years have been made by the staffs of companies, including audiovisual production companies, normally engaged in other work. In the distant past some film and filmstrip projects were done by teachers who dabbled in audiovisual production as a hobby. However, the product has become so sophisticated that almost no individual can complete such a project.

If the educational film and filmstrip companies can manage to make a good- to excellent-selling film or filmstrip set that the schools will buy in 1000 to 5000 quantities, the profits are enormous. The cost of film materials, in terms of the final print alone, is about 20 percent, and the selling cost can be as little as 10 percent but is more typically 20 percent. This means that an educational film can make 60 to 70 percent gross profit, and where typical prints are selling for $250, the potential is $1.25 million with $875,000 profit. The production budget for a film in this class will rarely exceed $30,000, so the incentive is high. Sales figures of this kind have happened, but they are the exception and not the rule. Many educational films do not sell at all, and many sell only a few prints per year. The educational film companies have to make it on averages, and in most cases they won't know the outcome of their decisions for three years.

The educational filmstrip business is a little different. The production cost of a top-quality set of six filmstrips is now $15,000 to $30,000. The set sells for about $100, and 1000 to 5000 sets should be sold over a 10 to 15 year period; thus, the gross could be $500,000. In this case the cost of materials is only 10 percent, and the selling cost varies from 10 to 20 percent, so the gross profit potential is in the $300,000 to $400,000 range. In the past, educational film and filmstrip companies were willing to give a producer a 12 to 15 percent royalty on projects that he developed and produced for them. But, they have become both cautious and greedy of late, not wanting to spread their inventory dollars too thin and not wanting to pay the royalties for the next decade and beyond.

Any decent filmstrip should sell for $10,000 to $15,000 on a buy-out basis with no royalty interest, and an educational motion picture should be in the $60,000 to $90,000 price range. At this time none of the educational film distributors seem to be willing to spend this kind of money, and many of their films are now made by students fresh out of school and able to live on little money. These young producers will make one film on an uneconomical basis, an advance of $15,000 to $20,000 with a small royalty, and from this start they either may or may not make it in the business. Occasionally, a young producer will come along with an incredible talent, make a film that goes off the charts, and actually make money on a five percent royalty. If he's smart, and these young producers usually are bright, he will get a better monetary deal the next time around.

The economic reality of the educational film and filmstrip business is that it produces initial sums of money that seem large, but are not, and the pay-out is over such a long period of time that most producers cannot afford to be in this business. Since the sales potential is so incredibly great, you would think that more young producers would go directly into distribution and make the money themselves. This can be done and the numbers are exciting, but the risk is great, and you have to pour a lot of money into the equation to even find out if you're wrong.

We have our own distribution company for educational filmstrips, and the total investment involved was $100,000 before we got the enterprise going properly. This was only after I had been in the business for 16 years, had a fair idea of what to do, and was fairly well known to the schools. Approximately half of the schools to whom we were advertising had already purchased one of my filmstrip sets from a major educational distributor and could find my name in any of their catalogs. This gave me credibility in the marketplace and today that is especially important. There is a lot of money to be made in distribution, but it takes both money and time to work into it. Distribution is not a field for a beginning producer.

PRICING

Setting prices is a very tricky problem in audiovisual production. Most clients want to know *exactly* what a job is going to cost, and few will agree to a time-and-materials open-ended arrangement. You have to remember that a price is simply a way of getting together. If the price doesn't work, high or low, there is no law that says it can't be changed. However, there is a tradition in business that "A deal is a deal," and with some clients this axiom is law.

My own research into the pricing practices in audiovisual production showed such a wide range of information and attitudes that I had to develop my own theory of pricing, and this has worked so well that it seems appropriate to pass on. The distribution of incomes in this economy is such that twice the median figure is in the upper 10 percent, and three times it is in the upper 5 percent. The shape of the income distribution curve is such that it appears quite easy to move from the middle to the upper 10 percent and difficult to move upward from that point on. Thus, I estimated that if I were to price my work to put my income in that upper 10 percent, the figure would be both competitive and convenient. To try to push my figure to the very top would probably be counterproductive.

In 1978 the median income was about $12,500, and thus the two key points on the curve are $25,000 and $37,500. Breaking these figures down to an hourly wage produces $12 and $18, respectively. When I priced jobs according to this range, there was never a problem over money either in getting paid or having the client return. Of course, any expenses, equipment rentals, and so forth, have to be added to the cost, but pricing in accordance with this general formula will keep you competitive.

There is a persistent danger of pricing yourself out of the market. I have personally witnessed this twice. In one case an excellent photographer who had been on the masthead of a national magazine quit his staff job, built a fine studio, and got a lot of work quickly. Within three months he raised his price to a whopping $1000 per day! Then, he wondered out loud where all the clients had gone.

In another case, this one concerning a cinematographer, the man had been working night and day for a daily rate of $150. He suddenly became greedy, apparently thinking all the other lensmen in Hollywood had died, and escalated his price in $100 increments to $750 per day. Suddenly—no more clients. It is a rare client who will tell you your price is too high. They usually go somewhere else quietly. In both of these cases it took many months for these people to get rolling again. There are other ways of pricing and handling business that can bring higher yields.

When you are just starting in the audiovisual business, there are many confidence crises over your own ability to complete a show, and there is much wondering about how much time it will take. As a general rule, it seems that if you figure how much time an operation should take, whether it be a shot, sound job, titling, or programming, and multiply this time by 2.5, you will arrive at the amount of time involved. The temptation to try to get the client to cover your lack of confidence with a blank check (a time-and-materials open-ended agreement) must be suppressed or eliminated. It is far better to give him a solid price for the job and just be very efficient when doing it.

In this work there is no substitute for experience, and your ability to analyze a situation and estimate how much time and expense it will require is a function of that special knowledge. A few years ago I was asked to produce a series of filmstrips for the Sea World organization. The contract writer-producer was very nervous about the project because underwater photography is one of the most difficult and dangerous types of photography, and therefore is also not inexpensive. Because I had a lot of what she needed in stock and had a desire to obtain the rest anyway, I offered to do the job for the $25 per picture she had in her budget on a *single-use basis*. They would copy the images onto the filmstrip internegative and return them to me.

The project also included a considerable amount of exterior beach and tide/pool photography, and where some photographers would be hesitant to make a fixed bid on this work, I did it in confidence. The edge of the sea is a special place in terms of weather, clouds, and the light needed for photography. It can be difficult to get the kind of day you need, and if anything goes wrong you will rarely be able to match frames in a sequence. The entire sequence will have to be redone. The fact that I knew the locations so well relieved me of this problem, as I could previsualize all of the pictures in the script after the first reading. In addition, there is a location near Point Dumé where I have never seen a totally cloudy sky for more than an hour. Apparently, there are some sea, land, and wind phenomena there that break up overcast conditions and produce attractive skies. Fifty frames of that kind of photography were needed. We did it in one day, paid the young model $25, and netted $1225.

If I had told the client that I would have to do this work on a time-and-materials basis or needed so many days for the beach and tide/pool sequences, and so forth, and so on, the project likely would have been killed, or someone else would have gotten it. In all truth, I did not make out very well with the underwater material because we had to make many trips to get it. However, the project was well worth the price I was paid for it because I own the pictures.

This brings us to a very important point in audiovisual economics. *Always sell your images on a single-use basis.* You may never sell many of them again, but those that you do sell over and over again will make the collection well worth maintaining. We normally sell 35 mm slides for filmstrip use for $25 to $50, depending on how many are purchased. Of the 30,000 images we now have in stock, perhaps only 1000 have been sold at all, but some of them have been sold many times. However, in one sale the final figure was over $15,000. The frequency at which we rent the images is purely a function of how hard we work the collection. This is a side business that does take a constant effort and some advertising, but it can pay off if the photographs are very good.

Pricing in the areas of show production depends very much on the medium for which you are producing and the source of the images. If you are making a simple dissolve slide show with stock production music and a narrator, and much of the visual materials are supplied by the client, as a ball-park figure the price can be $400 to $500 per running minute of program. If your expenses are normal, you should come out with about 50 percent gross profit and probably feel adequately or well paid.

A filmstrip has to cost more than a simple dissolve show first because of the internegative preparation, which alone will cost $400 to $500. The filmstrip also may require more photographic production than a dissolve show because the medium is very limited, is static unless handled carefully, and there is a format change when going from 35 mm slide to the filmstrip aperture. The style of filmstrip production has changed markedly in the last few years and now calls for elaborate posterizations, special imaging, special graphics, and optical tricks. All of this adds up to higher final figures than those of a simple dissolve show, and now we figure commercial and educational filmstrips at approximately $1000 per running minute.

If you are doing a series of filmstrips, there will be certain economics in the production, but one of them should never be the multiple use of a few images to the point that it becomes obvious. The real economies come in multiple use of sets and locations, as well as talent, in a way that will make the cost of each filmstrip drop dramatically. If these shortcuts work out well, you can cut the series price in half and again be at the $400 to $500 per minute figure that used to be the standard of the filmstrip industry.

A 16 mm motion picture can have a cost little more than that of a well-prepared filmstrip ($1000 per minute), as many of the techniques are the same with only the camera and film stock comprising the difference. But, more typically, the 16 mm film will have a budget two to four times that of a filmstrip, i.e. $2000 to $4000 per minute of finished film. Motion-picture budgeting is both an art and a science complicated by the difficulties of having a shutter that cannot operate at speeds less than 1/48 sec. and the problems of making a 4.5- to 91-kg (10- to 200-pound) camera move smoothly and well. The high speed of the motion-picture shutter requires vast amounts of light unless grainy high-speed films are used, and the mechanical difficulties of camera movement are horrendous. As a result of the problem of camera movement, the production of high-quality motion pictures has become an engineering field in its own right.

Video production began as a rather inexpensive way to make motion-picture-type shows. Video production was initially black and white, which simplifies much of the set design, painting, and decoration problems. The quality of the acceptable image was so low you could get away with murder in special effects. The shows were directed and edited "from horseback," as the directors say, all in real time and usually after one rehearsal. The perfection of the color process, improvement of the electronic image, and videotaping and editing now have brought the cost of videotape production up to that of the film process. In general, the ¾-inch process has a price comparable to that of the 16 mm, and the pricing of the 2-inch process compares to that of the 35 mm motion picture.

Entertainment motion pictures can have prices ranging from $1000 to $100,000 per minute of finished program, and even more in cases in which high-priced talent has been used and the production has gotten out-of-hand. The low-price category includes the x-rated films shot on a few weekends in motels, homes, and the streets of Hollywood, the nature films put together from stock shots or done in foreign countries, and stock car and motorcycle pictures seen in back-country drive-ins.

Entertainment productions have become a fashionable form of investment or tax shelter, although the Internal Revenue Service has been bearing down on some of these projects. It is possible to set up a proper corporation for such projects, take huge tax losses, and even have some fun in the process. If you have one business that is making a lot of money, giving you an income in the 50 percent or better tax range, these kinds of investments can be interesting because your potential loss is diminished by your tax situation. However, your potential gain is not diminished in the same way. Physicians, professionals, and businessmen are the favorite kinds of investors in these kinds of projects. Most will do it once and not return to the film investment game unless they make money at it.

The illegal part of this business is the production company that never gets distribution for its films or television shows, but makes them year after year, losing a lot of other people's money. The various producers and executives are paid handsome salaries in the process, but nothing ever seems to make it to the screen. The tax and law enforcement people have put some of these people out of business, but there are many who continue to operate just inside the law. The numbers are always large in the entertainment motion-picture business, and it causes a fever of a kind rarely seen in business. This is a field that one must enter with caution, knowledge, and professional guidance of only the very best kind. If you ask enough questions, you will eventually begin to hear the same correct answers over and over again.

THE FUTURE

The audiovisual field has an incredible future because the public is not yet fully aware of its power, impact, and value. Business is just becoming aware of it and is spending money virtually like water on audiovisual projects. The home market has just been tickled and never tapped, but all of this will change soon. Videotape recorders are probably the hottest new product on the market, but the machine that will cause the revolution that we would like to see is the video-disc machine. DiscoVision, a subsidiary of MCA/Universal now merged with N.V. Philips Gloeilampenfabrieken, is based on a process that uses a modified mirror disc spinning at 1800 revolutions per minute. At this writing, each 12-inch disc contains 54,000 grooves, and each groove contains one picture and the sound-track information for $1/30$ sec. Played in the normal television mode, this gives 30 minutes of program per side of disc. The disc can be rolled and mailed in a tube and has a manufacturing cost of 40 cents. In operation nothing touches the disc but the precisely aimed beam of a laser. The pattern recorded in each groove modulates the reflected beam to produce the information that results in picture and sound. Any of the individual images can be recalled, or the program can be played in the normal manner.

The video disc could bring the end of the printed page in many media. All of the information in many books could be stored on one disc at a fraction of the book production cost and in a much more permanent fashion. It is now becoming apparent that a book is a temporary thing, and most of the major libraries are recording their books on 35 mm film before they crumble to paper dust. Conversion to video disc would be just as permanent a method of storage. It is quite something for a new process of this kind to result in a more permanent record than what we have seen, at any price. But, the fact that this process is so very much cheaper than anything previously seen is the signal that we are truly about to enter a new information and communication age.

The economics of the video disc cannot yet be determined because the product is too new and its marketing has yet to take shape and happen. The best parallel in our history is that of the LP (long playing) record, which came on the market in 1950. Not only does the LP record look like the video disc, but it also had to compete with existing technology, and its players cost substantially more than the existing equipment of the day. But, the LP was a breakthrough in terms of quality and usability. The complete conversion of the record industry from 78 r.p.m. records to the 33⅓ LPs required 10 years, which is an understandable period of time when you consider that the LP was fighting a well-entrenched industry and its own manufacturing and distribution problems. There were times when the new record players, amplifiers, and speakers were not available due to excess demand. Economically, this not only slows the sale of the product, but also drives up the price, increasing consumer resistance to a wider segment of the market. It also confines the perimeter of exposure, which will slow sales.

There are 65 million households in this country, and 50 million have at least one record player. But all of these same households have television sets. Several marketing experts have been noted as saying that they doubt it will take the video-disc industry more than five years to make a total, or near total, penetration of the home market. This is, of course, assuming there will be no manufacturing and supply problems to interrupt the flow of players to the market. Such interruptions in availability cause waste in marketing and advertising efforts and make effectiveness hard to determine.

The most exciting feature of the video-disc potential is in opening the home market to audiovisual producers. We now have thousands of programs in the forms of educational, industrial, and special-purpose motion pictures, filmstrips, and video shows that could be converted quickly to the video-disc format. Whereas the disc itself can be struck for 40 cents once the stamper is made, the show should be salable for a few dollars, if it is existing material or if it is a show of the low-budget type now being made by most small producers.

The video disc is virtually indestructable and is not in any way worn by use. This should make the product of great interest to schools and public libraries, where shelf life is an important quantity in their equation. Librarians are continually looking for products that have wider appeal, and the video disc could be the invention that gives libraries universal appeal. The primary difficulty with books is that it requires effort to extract usable information. The video disc, like any audiovisual program, requires little or no effort to use, and this alone will broaden the appeal considerably.

The video disc is also the big-budget motion-picture producer's dream because it has complete integrity and can be obtained only from the original stamper. The discs cannot be recorded in the home because the player does not have a record function, and while it may be possible to copy a video-disc program onto a blank videotape cassette, the cost of the blank cassette will likely continue to be more than the cost of an original video-disc program. The mastering and stamping machinery required to make video discs is now expected to have a cost of $100,000 to $250,000, far too large a sum for anything but a professional lab.

If the video disc has only as good an acceptance as similar types of products, and it is expected to do far better, the potentials would be 5000 to 10,000 sales per program for the school market, a similar market in the public libraries, and a half-million-unit market in the home. In each case years of marketing effort would be expended to achieve full sales potential. None of these sales will be accomplished overnight.

Some artists feel that it is unfortunate that economics has to play such an important part in creative fields. However, it does, and it is very much a part of the problem. All of the successful people that we have ever seen in the various audiovisual fields have had an intense curiosity about business and economics. It makes no difference whether you work independently or for the largest corporation in the business—decisions have to be made for economic and artistic reasons. Easily half of the success of any audiovisual project depends on economics.

4

The Script

If you were to walk onto the set of a major motion picture, television show, commercial, or educational or industrial film or filmstrip, you would find one element common to all of these productions—the script. In all cases the script will look much the same, as it is written in scenario format, which contains scene descriptions and audio lines or narration. In addition, the scene descriptions will include sound effects, music, and in some cases, the amount of time the visual or sound will be seen or heard. Reading scenario format is an acquired skill, and an amazing number of people in management positions in the audiovisual business have not mastered it. Very few "civilians," as motion-picture people call those not in the industry, are able to read scenario effectively. Thus, in the cases in which you are doing a production for a business client, you should probably present the script by explaining and playing the parts yourself. Or, you may be able to give the client an abbreviated version of the script so he doesn't become bogged down in set, prop, and production details.

WRITING SCENARIO

If the number of people who can read scenario is small, the number who can write it is microscopic. Apparently, the reason for the latter difficulty is that these media do everything for the audience, giving them sight, sound, and word. While writing a scenario is complicated, involving handling three or four channels of information simultaneously, it is the most powerful and lucrative skill that anyone can learn in the audiovisual business. Script prices range from $500 for a single filmstrip script (these are written in groups of four to a dozen for a series and from a single body of research) to $100,000 for an original screenplay. Many screenplays have been sold for a few thousand dollars, and the price for entertainment motion pictures varies widely, depending on the original source and the nature of the story. Educational and industrial motion-picture scripts usually run about $100 per minute of final running time. However, the real money in writing your own material comes from also producing it. The responsibility is greater, but the efficiency tends to be higher and the profits greater.

It is virtually axiomatic in the audiovisual business that every project will manage to have one horrendous hang-up that will threaten the completion of the production. In almost every case the difficulty is traceable to the writer, and generally, if he looks into the problem, it will be due to faulty research. It is extremely helpful if a writer has had an early background and long association with the subject matter of the production. Occasionally, someone new will bring something fresh to a subject, but generally, writers are better off working in areas in which they are not only prepared but experienced. I have written out of my subject-matter field on many occasions, but not efficiently. If the scripts turned out well, which I believe they did, the price was excessively high in terms of time. Staff writers can sometimes afford to spend months working on a single script, but a freelancer cannot. I knew one staff writer who spent two years working on a single motion picture on alcoholism, yet when the time came to photograph the basic fermentation scene, he was amazed to see nothing happen when all the ingredients were mixed together. I got his frantic phone call from the sound stage, where he had expected to shoot the scene in a couple of hours. He nearly died when I told him the reaction he had set up would take one month to complete. If management feels that their man, regardless of his background, should do a job out of his field, they had better be ready to pay for it.

A beginning writer will find it impossible to get an assignment without a sample, and then he may have to write the first draft for his first client on a speculative basis. The sample can be on almost anything and should be within the subject matter in which the writer is prepared. A good writing sample can be circulated for years, and spending time on one will never be wasted unless the writer never submits it. Many people who decide early in life to be writers take college majors in English, literature, or journalism, but these backgrounds are not necessary to get into the writing phase of the audiovisual business. There are probably fewer writers of the classic writer's background in audiovisual than in any of the communications fields, but this is not to say that such training is unimportant. The audiovisual business is still in an early phase in which it is more concerned with converting material from the printed page to the screen than it is with generating original products. Thus, audiovisual script writers are needed in all subject-matter areas. Critics of the audiovisual industry and its effects on our culture, say that we are creating a generation of illiterates This is the unfortunate nature of progress; old skills disappear as new ones replace them. But, it is my own opinion that it is too early to conclude that audiovisual is killing reading. The percentage of people who actually do any substantive reading has always been small, and if book publishing figures are any measure, that percentage is now smaller than it ever has been. In the distant future we may well see the end of the printed page, and the end will come at the hand of the audiovisual writers. However, for the time being we who are contributing to the demise of words on paper must be masters of them.

WRITING FOR PRODUCTION

The audiovisual script is the map of the entire production. The script must contain every element of the production, making it possible for the producer to extract lists of every object, costume, location, prop, and person he needs to complete the project. This process is called *the breakdown.* It is a skill in its own right, and the subject of our next chapter. The freelance writer usually will not do the breakdown, but he must be aware of it and provide enough information for the producer to get it done properly. It is in the area of writing something producible that most of the serious script problems occur. In the most incredible instance of pure disregard for the problems of production I've ever seen, the writer of a biology filmstrip series on adaptation described the opening shot as follows: a boy standing by a stream in which a large fish is jumping for an insect; in the background meadow there are two elk that are being stalked by a pair of wolves; there is a large tree, fully leaved, but full of birds of every size and description; and there are several birds in the air. The first man who was contracted to photograph the series had done some filmstrip work but never an entire series, and he wanted to enter the business as a full-fledged producer. He became so depressed over the contents of the script that he actually became ill. Months were allowed to pass while he stewed over the scripts. The executive producer brought them to me for a "fix-up" job, frantic to have the series completed on schedule. After reading the scene description I said, "I'll give you the boy by the stream and maybe a bird in the air." The producer agreed.

The point of the original opening photograph of the filmstrip series was that there is an abundance of life on Earth. There are so many ways that this can be illustrated, which are far easier to produce, that it should be judged a crime to do it so very badly. Something as simple as one of the NASA images of Earth in space, which can be obtained free of charge, could be brought in progressively closer in three or four frames, while the sounds of animals and then people and children are brought in with lots of reverberation. After the title frame the sequence could continue with shots of animals in the forest, animals and people, people only, and so forth. Or, a collage of small reversal prints made from images within the filmstrip's individual frames would not only provide the opening sequence, but would relate to the image content of the entire filmstrip as well. It is not necessary to be a genius to do something simple and do it well, but far too many would-be writers in the audiovisual fields are obsessed with grandiose objectives.

Learning to do things that are producible is a great challenge in the audiovisual business, and it is one reason that audiovisual writers have to be involved with cameras and sound equipment. There is no substitute for knowing what a camera can and cannot photograph, and what a tape recorder can and cannot record. The entire sound process is so strange, unexplored, and wide-open, that it is the subject of another chapter in this book. However, it is a field that requires hands-on work. In this way you can learn first hand what the equipment is capable of producing. And audiovisual tricks are not the answer. The great danger in learning many tricks and gimmicks is that they may begin to dominate your work. If you get carried away with gimmicks, the result can be pure disaster and the ruin of what may have been a good script.

THE OUTLINE

A good script not only contains every element of the production, but it realizes every objective in the show outline. Ideally, there should be one or at least very few objectives. It is far better to teach one thing well than to clutter a program with too much content and have none of it absorbed by the audience. An outline will give your script a chance of turning out well, because the outline is the bare bones of the thing, the skeleton on which the flesh can stand. Once you have this basic structure down, there is almost no way the script can turn out to be a wandering, scattered thing. The first heading in my outline, under Roman numeral I, is always entitled "Preface." This is both the essence of the script and the objective, or objectives, in a single statement. Perhaps the best way to illustrate the process is to show an example. The following outline is from my filmstrip series entitled "Concepts in Photography."

"Lenses"

I. *Preface:* The human eye is a multi-focal-length system. The reason we use many focal lengths in photography is that these ways of seeing have already been a part of our experience.

II. How does the eye see?
   A. The human eye is a spherical camera with a focal length of 23 mm.
   B. The iris forms a variable aperture from 1.8 to 7.6 mm (f/13 to f/3).
   C. The area of sharp vision is only two degrees wide and is the same as seen by a 1000 mm lens . . .
   D. . . . but the total area of vision is 218 degrees, the angle seen by an ultra-wide-angle fisheye lens.
   E. The eye sees in two ways simultaneously.
      1. As a low-resolution, ultra-wide-angle detection system.
      2. As a narrow-field, high-resolution seeing device.

III. Apparently, we perceive in almost every focal length between ultra-wide-angle and telephoto.
   A. When we first enter a scene, the ultra-wide-angle portion of our vision establishes:
      1. We are level.
      2. We are not going to hit something.
      3. Where objects are located.
      4. The shape of things of interest.
   B. Then, our narrow-focus, high-resolution system scans the objects of interest. Scan order depends on:
      1. Needs.
      2. Brightness.
      3. Color.
   C. Our retention system then stores the images in a position and size reference system.
      1. If we eat the hamburger, it is removed.
      2. It may be stored as a memory. (That was a mighty fine hamburger.)
   D. Each image is stored in a way appropriate to its size and shape.
      1. These various "formats" are the focal lengths of our mind.
         a. The ultra-wide-angle tells us where we are in space.

      b. The medium telephoto tells us about the hamburger.

      c. The extreme telephoto picks out small, but important, bits of information.

   2. Thus, picking the right lens for a photographic situation requires the knowledge of whether:

      a. This is an establishing shot.

      b. This is an image to be isolated.

      c. The image is to be seen sharply.

      d. The image is to be remembered softly.

IV. Our distinctions of normal, wide angle, and telephoto are camera terms alone.

  A. The normal lens does not give a camera the geometry of vision.

    1. It only records an image in a convenient way . . .

    2. . . . with few distortions.

  B. The wide angle tends to give us images like those which place us in space.

    1. These images tell us that we are level, not falling.

    2. These images tell us where we are relative to other things.

  C. The telephoto lens gathers clear, high-resolution pictures of details.

    1. These are the decision-making inputs. (Do I want that hamburger?)

    2. Will I call that phone number?

V. Improper use of the focal lengths can be interesting or disastrous.

  A. Where am I?

  B. The giant hamburger!

  C. The biggest phone number in the whole world!

The script for which this outline was prepared follows the body of this chapter, and it will be possible for you to see how the bare ideas expressed herein were then fleshed out to make a whole presentation. Bear in mind that while the outline may look very comprehensive and rich with detail, it is dealing only with a few simple ideas, as the objective is to teach the fact that our use of several focal lengths in photography extends from the nature of human vision. This is a guiding principle in the use of lenses, and it is of more use than a great number of facts about the number of elements, *f*-stops, focusing ranges, depth of field, width of field, and height of field of the lenses in various applications.

You should also notice in reading the script that the outline is *not* an iron-clad contract that cannot be violated. During the writing of any script or story, there will be small, but important, opportunities that will present themselves, and you should run with them.

In audiovisual script writing I have always preferred what I call the "rosette" pattern of development, wherein the center is the objective, you radiate through a set of data or evidence to build a bit of the case, come back to the central objective, back out into more data or information, come back to the objective, and go on through however many cycles it takes to utterly clarify the matter.

During the time you make the outline, it will be possible not only to chart the objectives, but also to get some feeling for the correctness of the medium. During one such exercise a short time ago, I was planning to do a filmstrip series entitled "What Is Music?" The outline went together well, but it became apparent after the elements were in place that this project would have to be a motion picture and set of filmstrips, or a set of motion pictures. The making of the musical sounds, especially with the simpler percussion instruments, too often involves motion to allow the static filmstrip image to carry the illusion. This realization probably saved me a lot of heartache a long distance down the line. I redefined the project, wrote the script for 16 mm, and have been circulating it to educational film distributors. To date there have been no takers, but at some point in the future, perhaps after some rewriting, there will be. Writing for the audiovisual screen is just that kind of business if you stick to it.

Preparing an outline for a script like "Lenses" is a relatively simple matter for me because of my physical and biological science background, as well as my long association with cameras and lenses. For me, doing things in other areas usually requires anywhere from a few hours to a few days of research and reading. The best sources that I've found are books, and I believe this is the case because an author must refine his own approach to a subject when doing a book. In addition, editors, of which there may be several on one book, usually improve the work. I have never had an instance where a real editor made a manuscript worse, but I have had a couple of filmstrip series ruined by subject-matter specialists who were given the editorial responsibility and blew it. In the few cases in which my research has uncovered a book that has not been as clear as I thought it should be, I have called the author on the telephone or made an appointment to see him. In a high percentage of these cases, I've come away wondering who wrote his material.

The *Reader's Guide to Periodical Literature* is an excellent research source because magazines tend to be a little more up-to-date than books. However, the quality and correctness of their information is not usually up to the level of most books. Magazine features and columns are done with great speed, and too many of the writers of these pieces make the mistake of working from a single source and not checking references. In my own work for *Popular Photography* magazine, the actual writing of my column seldom took more than a single day, but the research consumed as much as three days. In most cases the interviewing and research for a single column story should take one day, but sometimes things can get out of hand. Any topic that we did in the medical field, such as the use of the Storz endoscopic lenses, always took twice as much time as would a topic in any other field. Medical doctors are difficult to get to, interview, and quote. If you can get five uninterrupted minutes with them, you're lucky, and rather than make a definitive statement, they will point you in the direction of a reference book that is written in medical terminology. Doctors are the most difficult of all resource people, but they are also the most unavoidable in this type of research because most writers need one to translate their own literature when writing a medical story.

When you finally have all the information together and shape the outline, there is only one thing left to do, and that is to begin the writing. In audiovisual script writing it is not only desirable but I think quite necessary to begin with a "teaser." In the example filmstrip script there are five such frames at the very beginning, the title and copyright claim pop on for the sixth frame, and the program actually begins in the seventh. In education this is done to get the students settled, but I think this method is just as important in writing for adults. In the example script "Lenses," which follows, a typical teaser not only opens the program but establishes the location and some of the props used in the filmstrip. The first thing heard from the narrator is the preface from the outline. The same thought, or guiding principle, is stated in the final sequence ending the program. This is one of the main formulas to which I adhere in writing educational programs. This formula is necessary if the program is going to stand alone or be used in most classroom and course situations. I have written programs, which were to be used in conjunction with other materials, that were not developed in this way, but by themselves they would not stand alone.

The only other principle that I think a writer should keep in mind when writing any kind of script is that of keeping things simple. The idea of having many things going on simultaneously—busy backgrounds, flashing images, thumping soundtracks, and rapid, witty dialogue or narration—may be something that the writer-producer can force together over a period of several weeks, but its educational value is in doubt when the audience is going to see it in a 12- or 15-minute period. Entertainment programs have made use of the "super-pace" technique, but you will notice that it seems to come and go in an approximate five-year cycle on television.

Good taste and smooth production are never out of style, but frantic pushing in a program may be very "in" or very "out." If you are making a slide show for a single convention, showing an up-to-the-minute mode may be the thing. But if your program is going to have any longevity at all, it will have to concentrate on sound values, usable feelings, and information that people want. In the sample script that follows, these abbreviations are used:

CU—close-up;
ECU—extreme close-up;
FX—sound effect;
MS—medium shot;
MWA—medium wide angle;
SUPER—superimposition;
UWA—ultra wide angle;
WA—wide angle.

SERIES: CONCEPTS IN PHOTOGRAPHY; SCRIPT: "LENSES"

Standard Leader:

1. UWA, fish-eye view of the interior of a room that looks out onto a green lawn. A white tabletop is seen in front of the many-paned window, and on the table there are a telephone, a note on pink paper, a yellow film box, and a hamburger on a white plate. FX: The electronic melody "Reality" for 10 seconds.

2. CU of the white telephone. FX: Continue the track for 3 seconds.

3. CU of the pink note. It reads, "Call Janet, 456-9926." FX: Continue the track for 3 seconds.

4. CU of the film box, which is standing on end. FX: Continue the track for 3 seconds.

5. CU of the hamburger on the plate. FX: Continue the track for 3 seconds.

6. Darkened repeat of frame 1. SUPER: "Lenses" and the copyright information. FX: Continue the track for 5 seconds.

7. Repeat of frame 1 in normal exposure. FX: Track down and under.

Narrator:

"The human eye is a multiple-focal-length system. The
reason why we use many focal lengths in photography is
that these ways of seeing have already been a part of our
experience. How does the eye see? . . .

8. Art of the human eye, side view. We see the cornea, iris, lens, muscles and ligaments, humors, and retina, but there are no labels. FX: Track continues under.

> "The human eye is a spherical camera with a focal length
> of 23 mm...."

9. CU of the iris in the drawing. FX: The track continues under.

> "The iris forms a variable aperture opening from 1.8 to 7.6
> mm...."

10. CU of a pad of paper on which a man has written "23 mm focal length/1.8 mm aperture = *f*/13," and "23 mm focal length/7.6 mm aperture = *f*/3."

> "This means that in camera terms, the eye has a smallest
> stop of 13 and a largest stop of 3...."

11. CU of the fovea centralis in the eye diagram. It is differentiated by a shorter radius, giving it the appearance of a dimple in the retina, and it is a different color. An arrow points to the area. FX: Continue the track under.

> "The area of sharp vision in the eye is only two degrees
> wide, and it is called the 'fovea centralis'...."

12. MS of the art. The arrow is still in place, but now we see how the fovea relates to the entire organ. FX: Continue the track under.

> "This tiny area of the retina sees as well as the finest
> camera lens and film combination..."

13. Repeat of frame 1, which is somewhat soft in the typical manner of super-wide-angle photographs. FX: The track continues under.

> "... where most of the eye does not resolve very well at
> all...."

14. Repeat of frame 2, CU of the telephone. FX: Track continues under.

> "It is the fovea centralis that makes the images we see
> clearly..."

15. Repeat of frame 3, CU of the pink note. FX: Track continues under.

> "... the ones that give us information..."

16. Repeat of frame 4, CU of the vertical film box. FX: Continue track.

> "... and that we remember well...."

17. Repeat of frame 5, CU of the hamburger on the plate, but it is covered with a black mat that contains a hole that is 20 mm (0.8 in.) in diameter at the distance at which we see the hamburger (61 cm [2 ft]). We see only a part of the hamburger. FX: Track continues.

> "At the distance at which we see this hamburger..."

18. As above, but another section. FX: Track continues.

"...the fovea only sees part of it clearly..."

19. Multiple image, or synthesized scan, of the hamburger. FX: Track continues.

"... but the eye scans the hamburger to assemble a complete image of it...."

20. UWA shot, in the same room but from a different angle. We see the table and the four props.

"Thus, the eye sees in two ways simultaneously. First, as a low-resolution detection system...."

21. CU of the hamburger. FX: track continues under.

"... then as a high-resolution seeing device...."

22. Art of the eye with lines drawn to show its wide-angle and telephoto functions.

"Our eyes have a wide-angle capability of over 200 degrees and a telephoto function of only 2 degrees. Our telephoto field is like that seen by a 35 mm camera with a 1000 mm lens. But, because of the scanning feature our eyes can effectively produce an image of any focal-length lens, from ultra wide angle to telephoto. Let's see how it works...."

23. UWA view as we enter the room with the table and props. The camera may be tilted slightly. FX: Track continues.

"As we enter the room our ultra-wide-angle system tells us whether or not we are level, where objects are located, and how they are shaped. We will scan the object that is shaped most like the thing we need at the moment. If we're hungry..."

24. CU of the hamburger. FX: Track continues under.

"... it's the hamburger. If we have to make a phone call..."

25. CU of the telephone. FX: Track continues under.

"... it's the telephone. If we've been expecting a call..."

26. CU of the message. FX: Track continues.

"... we'll study the message. And, if we need film..."

27. CU of the film box. FX: The track continues under.

"... the yellow box is the first thing we'll see...."

28. Repeat of the UWA view showing the tabletop and the four props. FX: Continue the track under.

"Before we can grab the hamburger, dial the phone, or pick up the message or film box, we must store these images in a space-reference system. . . ."

29. Collage on a jet black background. On the left and in the same place, geometrically, as in the UWA shot, we see a square print of the telephone. Then, and also in its proper location, we see a horizontal print of the telephone message. Next we see a vertical print of the film box, and finally, a horizontal print of the hamburger. A gray silhouette of a man's outline, from the rear, dominates the center of the scene and is centered at the position of his right eye. SUPER: a Cartesian-axis diagram centered through his right eye position. FX: The track continues under.

> "Our space-reference system is three dimensional, and in
> most people it is centered just behind the right eye. If you
> are left handed, it may be centered just behind your left
> eye. . . ."

30. CU of the man's right hand on the hamburger. FX: Track continues.

> "You can demonstrate that you store these images in a
> space-reference system by touching one object. Then, close
> your eyes. . ."

31. CU of the man's left hand on the telephone. Vignette the outer edges of the frame to show that this is a recollection. FX: The track continues.

> ". . . and you will still be able to find the other objects
> almost as well as if your eyes were open. This means that
> you are storing these images, and this is an important idea
> in photography. . . ."

32. Repeat of UWA shot in front of the table. FX: Track continues.
> "Our ultra-wide-angle pictures establish *where we are* in
> space. . . ."

33. CU of the hamburger. FX: The track continues.
> "A medium-shot, or normal-lens image, tells us what kind
> of sandwich is on the plate. . . ."

34. CU of the telephone message. FX: Track continues.
> "A moderate telephoto picture tells us that this is a
> message. . . ."

35. ECU shot of the message. FX: The track continues.
> "And, a longer focal length gives us the important
> details. . . ."

36. Repeat of the UWA shot. FX: Continue the track.
> "In picking the correct lens in photography, we have to
> decide if the picture is going to be an establishing shot. . ."

37. CU of the film box. FX: Track continues.

"... an image to be isolated..."

38. WA shot of three or all four of the props. FX: Track continues.

"... or a display of the relative position of the elements in
the situation. This is a little different from what we have
defined as an establishing shot, but it is still a picture that
tells us where these objects are relative to one another...."

39. CU of a camera and three additional lenses. We see labels on
each—"Ultra Wide Angle," "Wide Angle," "Normal," and "Telephoto."

"Our distinctions of ultra wide angle, wide angle, normal,
and telephoto are really camera terms alone..."

40. CU of the 50 mm lens on the camera, hand-held. FX: the track
continues.

"The normal lens does not give the camera the geometry
of the eye. This is a common misconception...."

41. CU of the hamburger. FX: The track continues.

"The normal lens simply records objects in a way that is
convenient and a way in which we are used to seeing
many things. Let's look more closely at how the various
lenses work...."

42. UWA establishing shot of a chessboard in a woodsy location. It is
sitting on a white, painted plaster of Paris or baroque wooden pedestal. FX:
outdoors-type sounds, and in the distance we hear a harpsichord. SUPER:
12 mm.

"Ultra-wide-angle lenses, like this 12 mm fish-eye lens,
establish where we are in space...."

43. WA view of the same scene. The individual pieces are more
distinct. SUPER: 28 mm. FX: Continue the track.

"The wide-angle lens tells us where the chessmen are
relative to each other...."

44. MS of the board. SUPER: 50 mm. FX: Continue the track.

"... and the normal lens closes in on the relationships
between them...."

45. ECU of one of the pieces. SUPER: 135 mm. FX: Continue the
track.

"It is the telephoto lens that isolates the pieces..."

46. As above, but from a slightly different angle. SUPER: 135 mm. FX:
Continue the track.

"... and gives us the details about them...."

47. UWA, fish-eye, view of the board. We see tremendous distortion;

pieces tower over us threateningly. SUPER: 12 mm. FX: Series of low, ominous tones and electronically processed outdoor noises.

> "This is not a picture inspired by normal vision. It tells us
> that our face is on the chessboard! Something is wrong,
> and these pictures can be frightening. . . ."

Track out:

48. UWA shot, back in the original setting, of the hamburger very close to the lens. Around it we see the normal details of the room. FX: The original track. SUPER: 12 mm.

> "Still, we can use these very short-focal-length lenses in
> unusual, but totally appropriate, ways. There is nothing
> wrong in this case; the picture simply says that we are
> going to eat this hamburger. . . ."

49. Repeat of the collage in frame 29. FX: Continue the track.

> "Human vision covers a wide range and many distances
> in space. The lenses we use relate to our visual system, the
> way in which we see and the manner in which we store
> images."

50. Darkened shot of the above. SUPER: Written and produced by Adrian Vance.

5

The Breakdown

The script falls on your desk with the "thud" of a small-town telephone directory. Inside are the names of props, people, and places you will need to complete the production. However, you must determine the best way to go about this task efficiently and completely so you can be sure that nothing has been overlooked or underestimated. Breaking a script down and setting it up for production is perhaps the most pivotal job in audiovisual planning. Every minute you spend sorting and planning the production is multiplied in many minutes of work. If the breakdown is done correctly, the production will go smoothly. But if the job is done carelessly, something will go wrong. It is here that errors in the writing will first appear, and the producer will have his last opportunity to get the script fixed inexpensively. Any script changes that are made from this point on will result in having to throw away some of the finished, or near-finished, product. The breakdown must be done correctly, and that is why I have developed what appears to be a foolproof system for accomplishing it.

I have written most of the scripts that I've produced, so my own breakdowns were natural things, half in mind after the writing was finished. In doing another writer's script it is necessary to become almost as familiar with it as you would be with your own, and this means reading it several times, virtually committing it to memory. It is this kind of familiarity that will not only form the base of your work on the script, but will give you a chance to test the writing in your own mind. If something doesn't work, meet with the responsible party and get the snag ironed out. It is this kind of concerned, thorough production that brings clients back to your door again and again. Never feel that an approved script is an iron-clad contract that

Breakdown *in audiovisual production means listing pictures or* takes *to be made in the several locations. Each list is not only a guide for the work, but also helps in figuring out the cost.*

cannot be altered. It should not be altered without the approval of the client or producer in charge of the project, but often these people are not as knowledgeable about production as they should be and would rather be made aware of a problem than see the project go down in flames. Our earlier example of the opening shot calling for just about one of everything Mother Nature has lined up in front of a bubbling brook is an example of a glaring error that should be corrected by the writer. That photograph was not producible and should never have been specified.

CLASSIFYING THE SHOTS

Every shot in a production will fall into one of several classifications. When listing the shot categories, include certain classes of objects, props, and people. Head one sheet of ordinary notebook paper with the classification title, i.e. "Exterior—open field with cattle," and list each shot that falls into that category on the page. In addition, each succeeding page should bear the same title and its number, 2, 3, and so on, so that it does not become confused with any other page numbered 2 or 3. This may mean that you will have a substantial pile of these sheets—seldom more than 100 for a large film or filmstrip series—but they are much easier to sort, organize, and handle than any other kind of list. When the entire production has been broken down into a list of picture or shot categories, the number of photographs or *takes* should be printed at the bottom of each page. These numbers should then be added and totaled and should agree exactly with the number of frames in the filmstrip series or the number of takes in the motion picture or television program. Once these numbers agree, check them again, adding everything in the reverse direction. If that checks, there is almost no way you can lose a shot and not do it on location or in the studio. In an amazingly high percentage of productions in which this kind of procedure is not followed, the photographer must return to a location or studio to make one photograph or insert shot because it was overlooked the first time around.

OBTAINING THE COMPONENTS

When you know what you need, it is time to consider the time in which to obtain the components. If any of the shots are to be acquired from stock houses or especially governmental sources, the source should be contacted immediately. In both cases, especially the latter, allow plenty of time for a reaction and second and even third attempts at getting what you need. I have found that you can give the most precise description of what you want and yet have to send essentially the same letter several times, along with returning the first and second submissions, to get what you want from both private and public photo librarians. Where it would seem that dealing with stock houses is one of the last jobs a producer should have to do in putting a show together, it is the first. When stock houses do respond quickly, you will find that there is yet another reason for obtaining their images first. Matching color balance, brightness, and the flow of composition will guide your portion of the production. If the image that you are buying has an essentially warm color balance, you will not, in all likelihood, want to go to a cold, blue image in the next shot. Something transitional is more in order to maintain the general smooth flow of a good program. It is rare to find a stock image that will plug into a produced show as if it belongs there, but it is possible to alter your own work while it is under way and make the image fit.

Next, any previously produced art that you wish to use should be cleared for copyright and permissions, as this can sometimes be time-consuming. In most cases, art that has appeared in books can be obtained quite reasonably for film and filmstrip projects.

Produced materials are actually last on the list of things you should attempt to obtain, but within this category there are two major headings: interiors and exteriors. Inasmuch as greater control is possible over studio work than over exterior work, it is generally more reasonable to do the exteriors first, and then produce the interiors as the last phase of the work. Unfortunately, production doesn't turn out quite so simply, and usually the interior/exterior phase is a mixture of both. The reason for this variation from what would appear to be the best plan is that it is invariably better to photograph models and actors in as little time as possible, getting them in and out of the production quickly. In the case of very young models or actors, it is imperative to move fast and finish their parts before they manage to injure themselves; anything can happen to a juvenile model during a production. In addition, the only way you can be sure that an adolescent will look the same for an entire week is to put him or her in a bottle between shooting sessions. Since this is not possible, do everything—interiors and exteriors alike—as quickly as you can. In the case of adult talent, it may be possible to spread the shooting out over a period of time and take advantage of production economies, but I recommend against this, as it is better to rent a studio for a few extra days and let it be vacant while you're out on location than to increase the chances of having one of the leads get hurt. Also, be aware of the fact that it is a different matter for a studio owner to have a tenant who rents the facility for 30 days and shoots for 10 of those days, than to have one who rents for 30 days and shoots for 30 days. You can almost always negotiate a price somewhere closer to your figure than to his.

SCHEDULING THE PRODUCTION

When setting up a production schedule, it is imperative to allow a few days for filling holes and editing. It is not necessary to do final editing as you go, picking the exact photograph or take that will be used in the finished show, but it is important to see the material enough to know that it is going well, that the equipment is working correctly, and that the talent is working well. I've only really been fooled about talent a couple of times, and in these cases I have had to reshoot sequences with new people. Fortunately, I discovered my mistakes in the first moments of the shooting, paid the party off, and folded for the day. When this happens, it is far better to get out of the relationship than to try to keep it afloat or put up with it. This is one event that you cannot plan for in setting up a shooting schedule. It should never happen, and preventing it will be discussed in the section of this book on models and actors and actresses.

In spite of your best planning, every production will have one big snag. Be ready for it and try to keep cool. If you have people working for you or with you on a project, the fact that you are in control regardless of the situation is very important. Emotions run high in the production of audiovisual programs, whether they are simple or complicated, because there is a lot that is unnatural about it. I have seen motion-picture crews break out in fist fights no more than halfway through the production, and the film never recovered from the deep animosity that remained. I know, in looking back, that a cool head at the top of the heap could have saved the day and the pictures. The truly effective producers and directors in the audiovisual business always seem to have their vision extended and their sights up. They never wallow in the little problems.

6

Sets and Props

SETS

The opening sequence of your script calls for a medieval laboratory with authentic implements. What do you do? The first effort you should make is that of finding existing implements rather than making them, because it is usually cheaper to rent, barter, or borrow an existing set than to build one. It is possible to borrow sets, especially some really unusual types, because the people who have built them often want publicity and will only insist on the usual screen credit. This is more a barter arrangement, but it is not the limit of possible bartering in the audiovisual business. If the rental fee seems excessively high, don't be afraid to say so. Rental fees for locations are seldom arrived at by any specific accounting procedure. These are the easiest prices to talk downward, but avoid offending the owner.

A few years ago I had written myself into the problem of obtaining a medieval laboratory. I was doing two series of filmstrips for the Encyclopaedia Britannica Educational Corporation that were cast in three time periods in the history of physical science. I had seen photographs of such a reconstruction done by a large drug company, but the set was on the east coast and I was in Hollywood. It really would not have been worth it to move my entire production back there even for the set, which was a near third of the work. Also, I wanted some of the implements to be working, especially the furnace, and I was quite sure that the mock-up was not functioning. Whether or not reconstructions are capable of functioning is very important in the production of a motion picture, but less so in a filmstrip. If the drug company's set had been in the Los Angeles area, I would have approached them first with the idea of showing off the set in an educational production. In 99 cases out of 100 this will work, and when it doesn't, the owner usually has something in mind such as a spread of pictures of his mock-up. Inasmuch as the set will be lit and decorated with at least one model or actress or actor, it is a simple matter to bring along another camera or shoot a few extra frames.

In my own case, I could not find anything in existence that would work, and I really wanted to have something unique for the production. Research will often reveal that there are wide variations in the cost of what can be called "authentic" reproductions. Drawing after drawing of medieval laboratories showed that they consisted of anything from a few work tables in a barn-like building, some without complete roofs, to elaborate stone and brick structures lined with literally hundreds of glass jars and bottles and featuring a delicately shaped oven for heating flasks and firing crucibles. The elaborate glassware collection was out. Not only would it be extremely expensive, if I could put it together, but it would serve no purpose. Since I've viewed several thousand audiovisual productions in all the media, I've come to the firm conclusion that the simplest possible set is the best in every respect. A 19th century living room must be cluttered with trinkets sitting on nearly every flat space because that was the style of the time, but barring that exception, sets must be simple.

Thus, I planned to build my own medieval laboratory and outfit it with the bare essentials to avoid the confusion of clutter. The set would include a single work table 0.8 × 1.8 m (2½' × 6'), large enough for any experiment setup of the time. The walls would be white because the color is not only authentic, but it is also the very best color for a wall in a production set. A white wall can be quickly changed to any color by the addition of a projected beam filtered with an acetate sheet. There would also be a few massive beams of wood standing in front of the walls because this was the building style of the time. A second table would be in front of the back wall. This table would have a false brick front, a black stone-like top, and an oven and small furnace for firing crucibles, heating flasks, and so forth. The oven and furnace would be made to function long enough to allow us to get the pictures of fire.

The building of this set required about 10 man-days. We made everything from scratch, including assembling the tables from used four by fours because they were not only cheap, but looked distressed, as did most workroom furniture of the time. The top of the work table was another matter. For the sake of the photography and working on the table, we constructed the top from a sheet of particle board glued to a framework to give it great strength. One by fours formed the sides of the top, and the entire assembly was covered with contact paper in a wood-grain pattern. Contact paper is one of the miracles of our time as far as set builders are concerned. With a few rolls of this paper it was possible to make this one, simple table look like any of several wooden-topped tables or a stone-covered unit. We used another darker and more heavily grained contact-paper pattern to cover the 15 × 15 cm (6″ × 6″) particle-board beams that stood in front of the white walls.

In a typical photographic studio, which is usually a large barn-like building, the original walls are either made of concrete block or exposed two by fours and other unfinished woodwork. Thus, large flats made from 1.2 × 2.4 m (4′ × 8′) plywood sheets are set up and clamped together to form a corner of a room, with each of the walls running 3.7 to 4.6 m (12 to 15 ft) on a side. These false walls are usually set up 0.9 or 1.2 m (3 or 4 ft) from the actual walls of the building, braced securely in place, and arranged for freedom of lighting. Also, a window or door can be placed anywhere in order to agree with an existing structure, in cases in which the exterior will be shot on location and the interior done in the studio.

More and more of all kinds of audiovisual work is being done on actual locations because studio expenses have inflated, camera and lighting equipment are smaller, lighter, and more effective, and the great number of aircraft in the skies prevents good sound work anywhere, including in the insulated sound stages. Recording techniques designed to eliminate background noises work almost as well on location as they do in sound studios, and recently, commercial aircraft have become quieter.

The studio is still the best place to do image recording because you have the opportunity to keep things under control. The studio environment can be a life saver if you are working with nonprofessional or young and inexperienced talent. Setting up the studio for work with talent is an art. You must have a comfortable place for them to sit while they are not on camera, as well as a degree of isolation from the public that will permit them to get into the role and pay attention to what they are doing.

Buying materials for building a set can be complicated and expensive, but there is one guiding principle to keep in mind: Cheap is good. It may be wise to spend a little more on the more permanent flats from which your various walls will be made, but everything else in the studio is temporary and will only be used for a few days. Nonetheless, I believe in great strength. Stress every table or large implement with triangles, and attach every board with nails and white glue because it is not only expensive to have a table collapse under a rented prop and onto a model, but it is dangerous. Safety is critically important on sets because they tend to be dangerous when they're not well put together. You can have the leanest, cleanest set you've ever seen, but come in with the camera, lighting, and sound equipment, and it becomes a maze of cables, wires, and cords with heavy, hot lights on stands that may be 3.7 m (12 ft) tall, 0.9 to 1.2 m (3 to 4 ft) across at the base, and very top heavy. A small motion-picture studio setup is typically a three-dimensional equation for disaster. Insurance can be obtained, expensively, but if something happens, in most cases you can depend on having to obtain a lawyer to collect from the insurance company. If the insurance company can show that you were in any way negligent, the coverage is voided, and you may be stuck with paying a judgment for the rest of your life. So remember—build for strength.

Paint is one material that I've found you can seldom have too much of because someone always manages to put a mark on a wall or scuff a prop. I always buy gallons of paint, select colors very carefully, and buy the best rollers and brushes. A good roller or brush is really worth the higher price because the paint just flows from them. Drop cloths are one of the great material bargains, often costing as little as 25 cents for a 2.7 × 3.7 m (9' × 12') sheet of plastic. I buy plenty of them and use them to protect everything when painting. Don't forget to keep the extra paint and a couple of clean brushes on hand when the photography is being done. One swipe of the right color will cover the inevitable spill or scuff.

If you don't know much about building and feel timid about it, don't give up without an attempt. The people who serve the building trade, especially those in paint stores, are full of good, free advice and solutions to your problems. Always tell them that you're building a set for photography or motion pictures, that you want to do so-and-so, and ask what they would recommend. Soon you'll be told how simple it can be. Professional builders have permanence in mind and won't take the short-cuts that are appropriate in set and prop building. Take, for example, my building of the brick oven and furnace used in the medieval laboratory set. If I had had a professional brick layer put the units together, they would have been perfectly straight regardless of what I had told the person, and the bricks would have been so well stuck together that we never would have gotten them apart. In one of the more fun mornings of the production of "Investigating Matter" and "Electricity and Magnetism," the filmstrips for the Encyclopaedia Britannica Educational Corporation, I built the brick oven and furnace from a pile of used brick, which is the most expensive kind but attractive, and my own batch of mortar mixed in a huge zinc-coated bucket, and slopped onto everything. It was a rich experience and the units turned out perfectly.

PROPS

When your set is finished, you'll have to dress it with the appropriate props, and if you're doing a period production, this can be one of the most troublesome, time-consuming, and expensive phases of the work. The professional motion-picture and television prop houses are one solution, but often they are expensive, charging a standard 10 percent of the value per week. A weekly rental is usually the minimum, but on some occasions you can rent a large item on a daily basis. The values that the prop houses place on their items are usually astronomical and normally exceed current replacement costs by a large factor. It is considerably to their advantage if a client ruins one of their props and has to settle with them. I have heard of producers who went to the trouble of finding and purchasing a replacement unit rather than try to negotiate with the owner or manager of a prop house. Prop-house owners and managers are a special breed and are often difficult to deal with.

If it is possible, try to obtain your props from other sources. Antique stores and thrift shops are good sources for certain objects, and for modern items rental shops are often excellent. The Abby Rents chain on the west coast is good for almost anything, and there must be comparable businesses in every section of the country. In dealing with any rental concern, including the professional prop houses, the first few times you rent from them you will have to leave a deposit equal to, or nearly equal to, the value of the item that you are renting. Later they will trust you to return the items. The rental agreement that they have you sign is a collectable contract. If you ever have a lot of time, it may be instructive for you to read one of these agreements. You will soon see that there is no way that the rental company is going to lose anything.

Occasionally, you can find odd props in strange places. At the time I produced "Investigating Matter," I had to call on a college teacher for some inorganic chemical crystal samples to be photographed. While walking through one of the chemistry building's labs, I happened to notice an ancient balance sitting on top of a metal cabinet that must have been 2.4 m (8 ft) tall. The balance was virtually overgrown with dust, and when I asked my host about it, he looked upward with squinting eyes and said, "Oh, that!" as if he had found a long-lost friend. He told me that it was an antique balance in excellent condition, and at the time he and his staff moved into their new building, he couldn't bring himself to throw out this old instrument. I asked if I could borrow it for my production on the condition that I would clean it up, restore it to working order, and return it to him in two or three months.

Cinema Props is one of the leading prop houses in Hollywood. Most items are rented for one week at five percent of their estimated value.

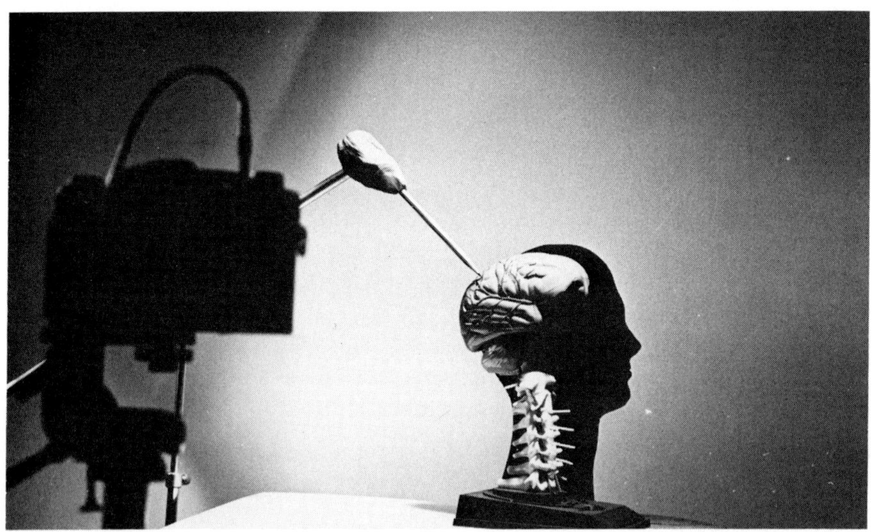

Flower Clay is an oil/clay mixture that remains soft to the touch. It can be molded and formed for many applications in the studio. Here it is used to form a "third hand" for the pencil.

Authentic props, such as this microscope model from the 18th century, add realism and interest to a slide show or filmstrip. Much of the power of media lies in its ability to transcend time.

He agreed and we climbed up on two laboratory stools to get the brass instrument down. It was very heavy and took several days to clean.

It would have been less expensive, in terms of time, to rent one of these instruments from a prop house, but none of the Hollywood prop houses had a unit of this quality. It gave the scenes in which it was used an unmistakable touch of quality. In another chance discovery during the same production, I found an ancient vacuum pump at the Los Angeles City School's Science Center. No one there could recall how it had come into their possession, and again, it was too charming to toss out. This unit, built from a virtual heap of instrument brass, curlicued cast iron, rosewood knobs, and handles, produced the most satisfying "slurp" ever heard from a vacuum pump. Another several days of brass polishing and painting put this unit back in working order. Although we only used it for a few photographs, the sight and sound of the pump set off the filmstrip completely. The point is you've got to constantly be looking for opportunities for getting and using props. If you make it a policy to return these antique units in better condition than they were when you picked them up, you will never have any trouble getting them. Both the balance and vacuum pump are now display items in their home institutions, and you can be sure that I could borrow the crown jewels of either place if I needed them.

Western Costume is one of the largest costume rental facilities on the west coast. It serves the motion picture and television industries almost exclusively. Audiovisual producers can rent costumes at facilities of this kind.

When you are renting props, you will soon find that there is a difference between the types that are functioning and those which are simulating. The functioning units, often necessary for motion-picture work, are more expensive, less frequently found, and more hazardous to use than the simulating units. In still photography it is rare that you will actually have to use functioning units. Whenever a group of producers get together, it is inevitable that the discussion will turn to some phase of the functioning versus simulating schools of thought, with a few diehards insisting that all things filmed should be actual. That would be a nice standard to have, but it seems unrealistic. In these two series of filmstrips in which I was being so careful to obtain and use appropriate, authentic props, we had to fake many demonstrations because the actual ones were so fleeting or subtle that they would either not record on film or the pictures would not be effective. I feel that the argument boils down to the fact that all film representations of

nature are themselves simulations, and for a producer to insist that everything that comes from the projector should have happened in front of the camera is silly. In the audiovisual business the objective should be to make the events that take place in the universe more understandable, and if we have to manipulate things a bit, that is just part of the job. The honesty that should be required is to know the phenomena actually work in the first place.

There are two instances I can recall that illustrate this problem and some of the difficulties of producing audiovisual programs in science. In one of my own productions for a large company we had a Ph.D. physicist acting as the consultant, and after reviewing one of my scripts he insisted that one demonstration would not work. I replied that I had done it, and that the thing actually worked that way, and so forth. He turned to a tablet of blank paper and set about making a series of drawings to prove that the script was in error. Nonetheless, I continued to maintain that it would work and that we could settle it with an experiment. Interestingly, he balked at this and patiently went through his series of drawings again. The conversation was taking place in an office attached to the studio, and as luck would have it, there was a PSSC (Physical Science Study Committee) physics textbook on the shelf. I grabbed the book like a man going after a life preserver and looked through the index for the heading. On the indicated page there was a series of photographs of a demonstration virtually identical to my own! My consultant accepted this, and if I had not been lucky enough to find it, or to convince him to look at an experiment, I probably still would be there trying to make his version work.

In the second case, which happened in the same studio, another consultant had the great brainstorm that the mechanism of a sea breeze could be demonstrated in a plastic box that was 15.2 cm (6 in.) thick and about 1.2 m (4 ft) square. In the bottom there would be a few-inch-deep "sea" on one side and dry land on the other. Heat lamps aimed at the "earth" would generate a higher temperature on the "land" and cause a convection current. Smoke introduced into the box would follow the classic pattern of rising over land and falling onto water, moving toward the land at the surface and away from it at the higher elevations. Simple as this sounds, anyone familiar with atmospheric physics and the radiation of the sun knows that the chance of making it work without augmentation is small.

This particular consultant was concerned with authenticity. However, no one pointed out to him that the box was about 1/10,000 the size of the smallest atmospheric unit in which the mechanism worked naturally, heat lamps do not make sunlight, and heat-lamp radiation would elevate the temperature of all the air in the box and not just that over the "land." In addition, the fluids in the box should have been scale-model air and scale-model water with molecules 1/10,000 actual size; you can't find those in a scientific supply house. And, water vapor from the land participates in the mechanism—not the smoke that was being injected into this microscopic atmosphere.

On the day that the demonstration was to be filmed, the studio was packed, and the temperature was 10 degrees higher than usual. On the first attempt the injected smoke rose a few centimetres from the tiny chimney and fell back to "earth." Some of the spectators and crew began to giggle, and the consultant moved nervously in and out of the center of interest sweating noticeably. After several attempts he remembered something that had to be done elsewhere and was not seen the rest of the day. The shot had been scheduled for a Friday morning, and I overheard some 50 takes attempted while I worked on props in a corner of the barn-like building. When I returned Monday morning, the entire apparatus was still in place, and the clap-stick slate showed that the last take had been number 147. At the rate they were working, they must have finally gotten it right sometime Sunday afternoon or evening. The producer and crew would not discuss the episode other than to say that they had gotten the shot, but there is no doubt in my mind that they must have augmented the effect. It would have been a relatively simple matter to set the air in motion before the camera was started, eliminate the heat lamps and their effects, and simply record the visual needed to make the point. This should have been the objective in the first place, rather than to stick to authenticity compulsively.

Getting ready for production can be time consuming and expensive, but it must be done with great care to be sure that equipment, talent, and rented studio space are not sitting idle while you try to make some recalcitrant prop behave. The next consideration in the process of production is that of light and its control.

7

Lighting

If there is a single secret to success in photography, be it still, cinema, or video, it is the control of light. By manipulating illumination you can make a room soft and sensual or stark and dramatic. Photography for reproduction includes all of the problems of lighting for effect in decorating stage or studio, as well as the problem of compressing the range of illumination so film can record it effectively. A photographic artist has to work with two different kinds of experiences simultaneously—his and that of his audience—all the while anticipating how film will record the scene he is painting with light. Most of the light in which we see is natural, but such light is not simple, and the photographer who insists on doing all work in natural light is sentenced to the bare opportunities of chance and the whims of a complicated environment.

Natural light consists of sunlight and skylight, in the main, but light from the sky may range from a cloudless blue source to one that is white (overcast sky). In this latter situation there are no shadows, and the photography can be incredibly simple: Find the right composition, aim, and shoot. This is the reason that England has long been so popular with cinematographers; the light source is generally an overcast sky. And yet, our own motion-picture industry is located in southern California, where light of the highest contrast found on the planet prevails the majority of the time. Of course the industry was located in southern California when even black-and-white cinematography required vast amounts of light. If there was any thought of moving to a location with softer illumination, the early color films certainly killed it. The first Kodachrome film, which was used in motion-picture production, had an exposure index of 10. And, some of the older cinematographers say that this was optimism on the part of Kodak, and that the actual index was closer to five. Now, with pushed color-negative stock, we have cinematographers regularly shooting interiors with estimated exposure indices of 1000 and 1200. I have heard of some experimental work being done at indices of 5000 and 6000, but these are not working numbers by any means. Still, high indices do not mean that these photographers disregard the principles of lighting. Quite the contrary. They understand the theory of lighting very well, but only handle small amounts of light to photographically create pictures.

To really understand light you have to start in space, and preferably at a place halfway between the earth and the moon. Earth has an atmosphere and the moon does not. In the distance the sun is burning brilliantly at the same level it has been burning at for several billion years and probably will for several billion more. Since the sun is 150,000,000 kilometres (93,000,000 miles) away, and on the earth's surface we can only move some one thousand kilometres in any direction, the sun is a constant light source. This is a very important fact for exterior photography, and it means that in a great number of cases you can forget about your exposure meter while photographing exteriors.

From our vantage point in space if we were to look at a desert area on the earth and a comparable one on the moon, we would see an incredible difference in the images of these areas, in spite of the fact that their components are nearly identical. The shadows on the moon are sharp, totally black, and nothing can be seen in them. The shadows on the earth are dark, but if you were to take an exposure meter into them, you would find that the light level in these shadows is fully one-eighth that of the bright sunlit areas on a totally clear day—one without a cloud in the sky. In order to make the difference between the light on the moon and the light on the earth totally meaningful, it should be expressed mathematically in a ratio called the *lighting ratio.*

$$\frac{\text{sunlight}}{\text{shadow}} = \text{lighting ratio}$$

In terms of footcandles the level of sunlight on the earth or the moon is about 7000, but in the shadow areas on the moon the level is zero and on our planet it is about 875 footcandles. Mathematical operations with zero are not defined, but it is a generally accepted idea that zero divides into any number an infinite number of times, and thus the lighting ratio on the moon is infinity. On the earth the lighting ratio is eight to one, and this is usually

Sun angle determines light level, contrast, and color temperature in most locations in California, where the atmosphere is usually clear and without interfering cloud cover.

A normal full-scale reading for an outdoor exposure meter with an incident light reading cone. Most exterior photography can be done with a single setting from such a meter.

Shade reading with an exposure meter shows that the light level is generally four stops below that of the open, directly lit areas.

the most contrasty light possible on the surface of this planet. The exceptions to this rule include those areas of a forest or canyon, where a single shaft of light often cuts through the darkness, and the ratio of the light approaches infinity. In most cases in which you deal with natural exterior light, the ratio is eight to one or less.

There are no clouds on the moon, and the light contrast there is always infinite, but on the earth clouds and haze in the sky change the natural contrast. As clouds or haze increase so will the level of light in the shadows, and therefore the lighting ratio falls. The contrast of light is extremely important to audiovisual producers because our materials are made for reproduction. The amateur photographer has the easiest job because he shows his product in its first generation. The professional is more concerned with how the final product will look, and that is usually a third- or fourth-generation print.

Reproduction processes have improved remarkably in the last 10 years, and today's professional photographers don't have to worry quite so much about the nature of original materials as before. But the same basic rules still apply, and while it is often possible for a processing lab to save the

Dulling spray kills excessively strong highlights in exterior photography and high contrast lighting situations. The spray will not damage metal or wood finishes, but test before use.

material, a patched-up job will never leap off the screen with reality. In essence, the photographic process has a range of four stops in the first generation. The same would be true in every succeeding generation if it weren't for the use of diffuse light sources in copy cameras. If you were to rate the contrast of this light, you would find it to be zero, like the white-light (overcast) situation. This light is used in reproduction because its softness hides dust and dirt on the film as well as scratches in the emulsion, but it also blurs all edges and fine detail. And, it does this in a nonlinear fashion, because more of this soft light passes through the highlight (thin) areas of the original than through the mid-range and darker sections of the exposure. Any detail in the folds of a white shirt or blouse, the texture of blond hair, or a place where a white background ends and a pale person begins may be lost in a reproduction made with a diffuse light source. For this reason most reproduction cameramen will pull the copy exposure down one to two stops to save these important details. The result is that the lower end of the exposure disappears into photographic mud, and the copy has that infamous dupe look.

You can alleviate much of this difficulty by reducing the contrast of the light in your original exposures so that the first-generation film contains all the important information in a range of two stops. This means that everything will have to be lit or filled unless you can do a lot of photography in situations in which there is a heavily overcast sky, and the light in shadows is no more than two stops down from that which is directly in the sun. If you ever have the opportunity to observe a professional motion-picture crew at work, you will soon see that most of the effort is spent in controlling the contrast of light. In bright locations a giant white screen called a scrim is used to chop the contrast of direct sunlight, and then numerous reflectors are aimed from the sides of the scene to fill the shadows with light. In the studio, hours will go by while the director of photography, grips (stagehands), and electricians assemble the components of a properly lit scene.

The rules in setting up studio lighting are exactly the same as in dealing with natural light. The guiding principle comes from the sun and sky, not only with regard to the ratio of illumination, but with regard to the direction as well. In the northern latitudes the motion of the sun is complicated by the fact that the earth is tipped 23 degrees. However, if the situation is simplified a little, it can be said that the sun rises at 6 AM and moves upward at the rate of 15 degrees per hour, since this is the rate at which the earth rotates. The apparent motion of the sun is quite vertical initially, but between the hours of 10 AM and 2 PM, it does not move very rapidly in a vertical direction. After 2 PM it begins to drop rather quickly, and on this ideal day under discussion, it sets at 6 PM. All of these times and angular distances are somewhat modified by the season and where you live on the globe, but the important principle still remains: There are four hours of increasing illumination in the morning, four hours of stable illumination in the middle of the day, and four hours of declining illumination at the end of the day.

Psychological studies have shown that people have their peak energy at 10 AM. They tend to be more involved and receptive at this hour than at any other time of the day. In the northern latitudes the angle of the sun at

The author adjusts a sun reflector to project light into a dark shadow for photography.

A commercial reflector can be used for either sun or flash projection. These units are light in weight but are sufficiently rugged to permit location use.

Close-up of a sun reflector fashioned from posterboard, a carved dowel, and a laboratory clamp. Such lightweight, portable equipment can make high quality production possible for a fast-moving audiovisual production organization.

this time is closer to 45 degrees than the 60 degrees the simplified explanation of the sun's motions would indicate. This is the reason that most knowledgeable photographers set their key light, the one imitating the sun, at a height equal to its distance from the center of the object of interest. Reading the level of this light, with no other illumination present, permits you to then set the level of the fill lights correctly to give a lighting ratio of four to one (two stops).

ACHIEVING NORMAL COLOR BALANCE

When the key light is set at a high angle, an imitation of midday sun, the color balance of the film should be normal. A normal color balance calls for equal densities of standard reds, greens, and blues. This is appropriate

*A "gobo" or "go between" is Hollywood's definition for a cardboard flag that is
used to control light. These implements are normally cut to a convenient
shape to form the shadow needed.*

because this is the normal balance of sunlight between the hours of 10 AM
and 2 PM when the sun emits equal amounts of red, green, and blue light. The
atmosphere acts in much the same manner as a blue filter, but the curved
atmosphere acts as a prism. Thus, the red and blue balance of sunlight is
changing from sunrise until 10 AM, and again from 2 PM until sunset. I believe
that this phenomenon acts as a kind of clock in pictures, and if you want a
photograph to have a certain time-oriented effect, the color balance of the
picture must be controlled to give it the correct quality. Fortunately, the red-
blue balance can be determined during the day, and the color balance of any
photograph can be changed in reproduction.

The red-blue balance is usually given in a term called *color temperature.*
In this system the base is the actual surface temperature of the sun (5600 K).

At this temperature the gases that comprise the sun's atmosphere emit equal amounts of red and blue. Green is omitted in this system because the green balance does not change in as significant a manner as does the red balance. And, our physical and mathematical systems can work much better with one unknown or variable than with two. It is not possible to lower or raise the surface temperature of the sun, but you can lower or raise the surface temperature of a piece of tungsten metal, such as in a light bulb, and observe the change in the red-blue balance. Also, these figures can be extrapolated, or extended beyond experimental limits and thus produce a system that carries the red-blue balance to incredible figures.

At sunrise, for example, the color temperature of the sun is said to be about 2500 K because it contains so much red light. If you read the actual amounts of red and blue light in the sun at sunrise, you will find that there is about six times as much red as blue light. This is very like the color balance of ordinary tungsten light in the home. An hour or so after sunrise, the apparent color temperature of the sun will have risen to about 3400 K, very like the color balance of studio illumination, with approximately four times as much red as blue light. The color temperature will rise rather quickly in the morning in most locations, and it will often be at the 5600 K level, equal red-blue balance, long before 10 AM.

In and around cities the color temperature of the afternoon light does begin to fall rather quickly after 2 PM, perhaps because of air pollutants, and by 3 PM it is typically at 4600 K. This means that there is twice as much red as blue light, and it is at this point that the change in the color balance can be seen. This can be a problem if you are out on an all-day shooting session and you want the color of the pictures to match and you also want the pictures to look as if they were taken midday when they were really taken early in the morning or later in the afternoon. There are two possible solutions to uneven color balance: One is to filter as you shoot, and the other is to color balance in reproduction. If your client is going to look at original material and is not knowledgeable about color balancing, it is best to do some filtration during the shooting session. If you are going to get into color-balancing filters for the camera, the best way to go is with the Tiffen DecaMired series. The series includes a set of eight filters—four red and four blue—in graduated densities such that they can be added to produce any needed density. When I first experimented with the system, I was concerned that using more than one filter would degrade the image. However, an extensive series of tests showed that this would not happen even with four such filters in front of the camera lens. The one very unexpected outcome from the test was that the resolution figures always improved when a red filter was used! The test was done outdoors in a situation very like that in which the filters would be used. This should always be the case in any testing program. Later, I found that the reason for the improvement was that the red filter was cutting out some of the natural haze in the atmosphere where the test was conducted. If I had done the test in a laboratory where the air is filtered and dried, or even worse, in a collimator where the light path is only a few centimetres instead of 50 focal lengths, this improvement would not have been seen.

I cannot overstress the importance of testing if you are working in photography. There is no place in this business for armchair engineers, but there certainly are enough of them. A simple test can save many failures. And, throwing money at a problem will not solve it. If you go into a photo store for advice about how to solve a complicated photographic problem, the person behind the counter may try to sell you the most expensive thing he has. Don't buy anything expensive unless you can take it back for a full refund within a specified time. I even have bought items on a 24-hour testing privilege, tested them, and returned them the next day. The easiest way to make this arrangement is to appear indecisive and then state your refund qualification. If this is agreed to, make sure the refund qualification is written on the sales slip.

USING FILTERS TO CONTROL COLOR BALANCE

The Tiffen DecaMired filters are easy to use and will solve your color filtration problems on the camera, as well as permit you to use indoor or studio film outdoors and daylight film with tungsten illumination. Generally, these are not recommended procedures and are only used in emergencies or for effect. If you use studio film outside with the DecaMired R12 filter, you will find the final product to be rather thin and often improperly exposed. I have never been able to determine why this is the case, but tungsten film used in this way seems to have about one or even two stops less range than when used with its own light. This effect is not seen when daylight film is used with studio lights and the B12 filter, but the strong blue of the filter makes the camera very difficult to focus and cuts the film speed down to one-fourth its original rating. I use this procedure when I want to unload a rather longish end of film in a camera, and there is some copy stand work to be done. In this very controlled setting where the shutter speed does not matter, the system works rather well, and I don't have to spend much time looking through the blue filter.

In professional photography most of your color balancing work will be done in the reproduction stage, and this work is done with a set of secondary color filters. The science of color seems incredibly complicated when you first become involved with it, but a simple device called the *color wheel* makes much of it instantly understandable. Segmented like a properly cut pie, this color wheel includes the three primary colors of red, green, and blue (note that they are each separated by one segment) and the three secondary colors of cyan, magenta, and yellow. The primaries are called primaries because they are the colors in which the film sees, and when projected they may be used in varying mixtures to make any apparent color. Also, these color filters block one another; a pure red filter blocks the transmission of green or blue light, a pure green filter blocks red or blue light, and a pure blue filter blocks red or green light.

Secondary colors do not behave in this manner. Projections of their light will not be interpreted as anything but the original hue, and when these secondary color filters are superimposed over a white light source in pairs, the primary colors result. Thus, if a magenta filter and a yellow filter

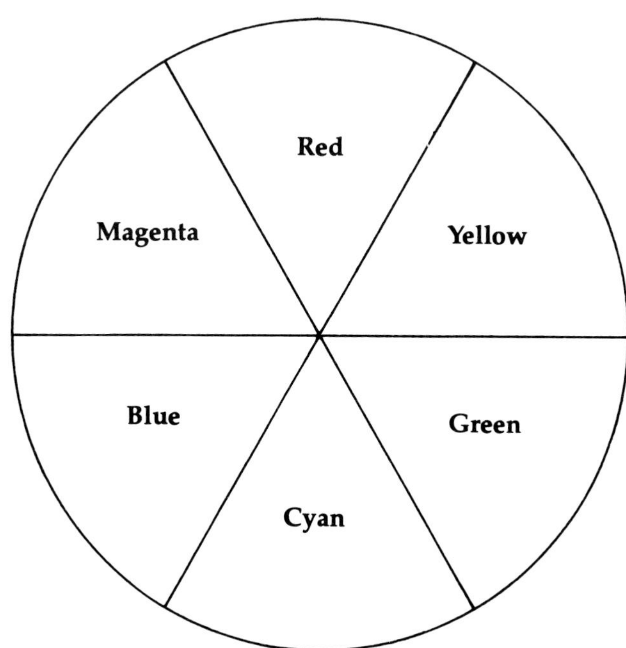

are held together over a white light source they will appear red, a cyan filter and a magenta filter will appear blue, and a cyan filter and a yellow filter will appear green. The secondary color filters block primary colors instead of other secondary colors. A magenta secondary color filter blocks green, a yellow secondary color filter blocks blue, and a cyan secondary color filter blocks red. The degree of blocking depends on the density of the filter itself and is graduated in a point system in which 30 points are equal to a transmission of 50 percent *in that color*. At this juncture the entire business must sound insane, but the point system is based on some very important mathematical relationships.

As you probably know, $10^2 = 100$ and $10^3 = 1000$. These powers of ten, as mathematicians call them, extend in both directions, and not only does $10^4 = 10,000$ and $10^5 = 100,000$, but $10^1 = 10$ and $10^0 = 1$. The interval between 10^0 and 10^1, the interval between 1 and 10, is of interest to us as the basis of the color balancing point system. As you also probably know, it was long ago discovered that an increase or decrease of 100 percent or 50 percent, two stops or one-half stop, must be made in a black-and-white exposure before a visible difference can be seen between two prints or negatives. This was the reason for the development of the stop system, wherein each camera or enlarger increment is a factor-of-two change, $2\times$ or $\frac{1}{2}\times$.

Meanwhile, the numbers between 1 and 10 may be expressed as powers of 10, and the number 2, for example, is equal to $10^{.30}$. That .30 exponent is 30 points. Thus, a filter labeled .30 and most commonly referred to by filmlab technicians as a 30-point filter will reduce the intensity of the light beam passing through it by 50 percent. These color balancing filters are usually sold in kits of seven in densities of 0.025 to 0.50. They may be added together to make any density up to a total of about 150 points in any one color. The most typical color correction ranges between 20 and 40 points and is usually in one color only. Corrections of less than 10 points are very uncommon. In addition, all three filters are never used together because the mixture of the three secondary colors produces a neutral gray, which should be subtracted from the filter pack. If you were to have a filter pack that included 30 points of magenta, 20 points of cyan, and 10 points of yellow, you would subtract 10 points of magenta, 10 points of cyan, and 10 points of yellow. This would leave you with a final filter pack containing 20 points of magenta, 10 points of cyan, and no yellow. As a general rule, you always use the simplest possible color pack in making color corrections. The reason for this dictum is that color filters are never totally pure, and the more you add, the more difficult it will become to make the ultimate correction.

As a typical color balancing problem, you have a set of slides with a slight greenish cast. This may be caused by the film being a little too old or overheated. This is one reason that I prefer to buy all film in bulk (several hundred feet at a time), freeze it, and shoot a test roll; there are no surprises when making this your operating procedure. But, should you be presented with greenish slides from you lab, the thing to do is to sit down at a light box, grab the color filter pack, and take a look at the color wheel. If the error is green and you can see it clearly, try a .20 magenta filter, putting it under the slide. If you still see any green, go to a .30 filter, and so on until the green is gone. If the error had been a bluish cast from shooting in open shade, another common error, you would lay a .20 yellow filter on the slide, and the error would likely vanish like magic.

The addition of these slides to a color pack will increase the required exposure, but remember that the filters act in a selective fashion and that 30 points of any color is not a reduction in the overall light intensity of one stop. In my own experience most of the slides that do have a color error are usually a bit underexposed at the same time, and your total correcting procedure may call for twice the normal exposure in reproduction. In this duplicating setup, for example, the normal exposure for a typical slide is 2 seconds at $f/8$, but slides that are being balanced for color errors generally receive a four-second exposure.

Color balancing may seem a little removed from exterior or studio photography and lighting problems, but it is something that everyone in the audiovisual production business should understand. The quality of the final product is the primary issue of your concern, and it is remarkable how much correcting and improving can be done in this final stage of the production.

This chapter began with the premise that if there is a single secret to success in photography it is the control of light. If you understand the nature of light—how it can be recreated in the studio with sources that do not move or change color by the hour, how the angles and colors of light control the viewer's perceptual clock, why fill light sources are so very necessary for work that is going to be reproduced, and the mechanics of filtration and color balancing—then you can make professional-quality photographs.

8

Vision, Camera, and Film

In the creation of audiovisual productions, one objective is to control the audience's perception of an event that is reported or synthesized. To that end, the mechanics and theory of photography and film are studied as if answers can be found in better knowing how lenses make images and how emulsions record them. But, such work can never help to design a better audiovisual program because it tells us nothing about the viewer's perception. Most of that perception is located in the visual process. How do we see?

THE NATURE OF VISION

Late in the summer of 1972, I was confronted with this question in connection with another project. The first place to begin any research project is in a major library, because this prevents repetition of work already done, and it usually helps you to shape your own approach. I was disappointed to find very little on vision other than in medical works dealing with structure and disease or basic descriptions of the kind taught in first courses in psychology or biology. There was nothing directly relating the eye and the camera, and this was my objective, as I wanted to develop a two-channel information theory for the investigation of events that had been seen and simultaneously photographed. So, the work had to be mine in the main.

A camera is more like a part of the human body than any other mechanical device. If you look at the human eye in terms of a camera, you will see that it is a spherical camera with a focal length of 23 mm. Light enters the eye through the cornea, passing into a gel called the aqueous humor and then into the spherical lens. Next, the image-forming light passes into another gel, one of a more viscous nature than the first, called the vitreous humor, and finally lands on the retina. The retina is a granular surface where each grain is a light receptor. There are typically 137 million receptors on each human retina, but most of them (130 million) are rod-like in shape and only detect light or dark. The remaining cone-shaped receptors are known to be the color receptors, and the information from these rods and cones is carried from the retina to the brain on a nerve bundle having only 800,000 fibers. How this bundle transmits the information from 17 times as many receptors as it has fibers has been one of the mysteries of vision, as well as an indication that there is a visual code.

The fact that there is a visual code is very exciting to anyone working with the theoretical aspects of audiovisual production—the design of new film and projection systems. A full breaking of the visual code, and an understanding of the visual clock and its cueing impulse, will mean that we will ultimately be able to transmit three-dimensional images electronically with a system perhaps less complicated than our present color television. The present color film system is an example of a partial breaking of the human visual code. Color film only records in the three colors of red, green, and blue, and we see all colors in terms of these three colors. Dr. Edmund Land has succeeded in making a successful "full color" process with only two colors but with a very careful control of the intensity of the projection. Land's two-color process will not work for reflection-viewed images because the illumination level cannot be controlled. Still, the most exciting of these processes is the simplest to construct and use, but the most difficult to understand. The toy known as Benham's Top (Benham was an obscure English monk) represents more of a breaking of the visual code than color film or television because it uses no color. The top can be made from lightweight posterboard with a toothpick passing through the center. When spun in a clockwise direction just fast enough to make the lines and zones merge visually, the outer ring appears to be red, the next inner ring green, and the innermost ring blue. If the direction of spin is reversed, the red and blue switch positions, but the green remains.

My own numerous experiments with various designs of this top, using every kind of dot, curved line segment, and so forth, have indicated that Benham's design is ideal. He undoubtedly did a lot of experimental work himself, but as best as I can determine, he did no interpretation. My own interpretation is based on the idea of breaking the disc into six segments so that the smallest feature of the face, any of the three lined areas, is one-

Benham's top may appear to be a toy, but it gives us several important clues about the nature of vision.

sixth of the circle. Breaking each red signal into its parts would then give us gray, white, white, black, black, black, where the gray is the lined area. The other designs that I tried, including various grays in that zone, indicate that 50 percent gray is one of the elements. The green signal is then white, gray, white, black, black, black; blue is white, white, gray, black, black, black.

If the visual code is based on a six-bit "word" with a three-element alphabet of white, gray, or black signals, then there are 3^6, or 729, possible combinations of these elements. Other of these "words" could be used to give the location of the image element on the retina, the intensity of the light on the receptor, and any one of a number of characteristics of the image. Such coding would be needed to permit the optic nerve to carry much more information than it has channels, as well as place the information in some usable reference. The visual process itself is not understood. Where is the image seen? We will later approach that question, but we first need more information.

Another characteristic of vision came out of the top spinning excercises when I observed that the top would appear to flicker when it slowed down. Vision appears to be a continuous process. None of the reference materials I consulted spoke of a visual cycle or apparent shutter speed for the eye, but it seemed to me that seeing flicker indicated that something like a shutter was working in the visual process. To determine the nature of this system I rigged another circular card, half white and half black, much like Benham's Top but without the sets of arc segments. This card was attached to a motor shaft which also drove an 80:1 gear reduction drive, and the turns of that shaft could be counted easily to determine the rate at which the motor shaft was spinning. This device showed that in bright sunlight I could see flicker at any speed below 50 revolutions per second. The rate slowed as the light level decreased, and in the darkest light in which the disc could be seen clearly, the effect of flicker did not appear until the disc's speed dropped below 20 revolutions per second. This change in the apparent shutter speed of the eye is precisely what would be expected as an accommodation to the change in light level.

When I determined the pupil size in the brightest and dimmest light in this series of tests and then read the illumination level on an exposure meter, I found that the retina has an apparent speed, in terms of exposure index, of 64 in bright sunlight and of 400 in very dim light. These ratings compare very favorably with those of normal daylight color film and high-speed black-and-white film. The *f*-stop range for the eye varies from *f*/13 in bright sunlight to *f*/3 in very dim light.

The geometry of the eye is such that it would be an ultrawide fish-eye lens/camera system if it is operated in exactly the same manner as the camera. However, vision is not that kind of experience. In addition, the only place where the eye is truly sharp, with a granularity of 100 cones per running millimetre and a performance as good as the better of the black-and-white films (about twice that of the best color films), is in a very narrow zone called the *fovea centralis.* This little spot in the center of the retina is only two degrees wide, seeing well in a field that is only as wide as a 500 mm lens on a 35 mm camera. The remainder of the retina has rods and cones distributed at the rate of something like seven per running millimetre, only enough to recognize shapes, but never bring them into sharp focus. Thus, the way an eye sees can best be summarized by stating that it is a viewing rapier surrounded by an optical detection system.

HOW VISION FUNCTIONS

The best description of the eye's function can be derived from our own interpretation of the function of lenses of various focal lengths. Traditionally, the 45 to 55 mm lenses are called normal lenses, and yet if you look at the structure of the eye, there is no way to justify that label. However, if this label is turned around and used for the important bit of information it contains, it may be seen that the eye functions in a scanning fashion over the approximate 45 degree field of these lenses. This normal scanning process is used to collect impressions of our surroundings, storing them in a way in which they may be used.

At this moment, as you read, you are surrounded by objects and none of them are sharply in focus because you are looking at this page. Your own field of crisp vision is so narrow at a typical reading distance that you can only see five-letter words clearly in one of the eye's instants—the smallest unit of its time. In bright sunlight your visual clock is producing about 50 of these words per second, and if you wish you can push along through these words at about 3000 per minute. However, most of us read at one-tenth that speed. The reason we read with such inefficiency is not because we are lazy, but because reading is an abnormal activity for man and a luxury of the moment, not the prime activity. Our eyes must tell us where we are in space, whether or not we are level, and the nature of our surroundings. The fact of the matter is that you can close your eyes at any moment and reach out and touch any of several objects in your surroundings with an accuracy almost as great as if you were looking at them. Why? Your visual process has given these things a place in space relative to you. Not just that place behind your right eye which appears to be the perceptual center for vision, but a place for every cell of your body. It is the job of vision to let every place in your body know where it is relative to everything around it. If you are relaxed and let the process flow, you will have a much easier time with such sports as skiing, where you unfortunately have to correlate three centers. Your visual center appears to be just inside one of your eyes, your center of gravity is at or just below your navel, and your center of contact is just in front of your toes on the inside edge of the ski that is lowest. What a mess. Although this correlation must come together more quickly than you think possible, when your visual process learns that toes and feet now have priority over where you are in space, skiing becomes second nature. In a typical learning experience of this kind, getting to this point can require 20 to 60 hours on skis. Still, knowing what the coordinating processes are should permit the development of a machine that will teach such things as skiing without the first chance of a fall. Perhaps one hour with such a device would permit students to go to the slopes and ski well the first time.

It is the ability to collect and replay reality that is the most exciting fact of the audiovisual business. The power of the medium is immense, and yet it must be handled with delicacy or the viewer turns off. We have to learn to think in appropriate sequences in most audiovisual production. The only exception to this is in the construction of a still image. Properly made, there is no such thing as a still image, unless you plan the displaying of it very carefully. At a normal viewing distance of 45.7 cm (18 in.) a typical 8" × 10" print actually becomes an information system containing as many as 200 bits. The print usually contains far fewer bits, and if studied may show a dozen or perhaps 20. However, the potential is there because the area of sharp focus of the eye is a circle that is only 18.8 mm (¾ in.) in diameter at this viewing distance.

When a viewer looks at a new image for the first time, he or she will almost always see the lightest object first unless the image is very high-key white with one or a few black details. Contrast is the determinant unless some strong motivating force such as sex, a female figure for males or a male figure for females, is also present. Sex is the strongest motivating force in any image, and studies have shown that the female figure will draw the attention of more people of both sexes than anything else. The single-bit print, in an 8" × 10" size, must be displayed where it naturally will be viewed at a distance of 6.1 m (20 ft), such as in the case of a gallery display that distance from a sidewalk or at the end of a hall. At this distance the image must be simple; a circular pattern or just a circle itself will work well because this is a suggestion of an eye, which is very strong visually. The well-known CBS eye logo is an effective attraction at incredible distances.

If you are planning to use a series of single-bit images on a screen, be sure that they are small. If the images fill the screen and the screen is much wider than two degrees, the eye will start scanning. The eye can only lock onto something that is two degrees wide. This angular width is 1.9 cm at 45.7 cm (¾ in. at 18 in.), the normal viewing distance for a print, 3.8 cm at 91.4 cm (1½ in. at 3 ft), 7.6 cm at 1.8 m (3 in. at 6 ft), 15.2 cm at 3.7 m (6 in. at 12 ft), and so on. If the images are of high contrast and the correct small size, you can effectively flash them on the screen at the rate of several per second. But if they are more than two degrees wide, the sequence won't work.

Thus, the eye is a viewing system that works in a series of modes, and one of these modes gives us a collective image rather like that seen by a normal lens. Within that field the eye is scanning continually and in any one cycle is probably hitting 12 to 20 of the possible 200 image-containing locations within that normal field. Initially, and periodically, the eye establishes itself in the location in its ultra-wide-angle mode of seeing. The view in this mode is like that seen by a 6.5 mm fish-eye lens on a 35 mm camera. This is the reason that each sequence usually must be started with an establishing shot, normally a very wide-angle picture of the area and usually one that is level. If the establishing shot is not level and is made from a low angle, immediately the message that something is wrong is projected. Or, if the establishing shot is one looking out from some odd place, such as through a stack of books in a library, the feeling projected is that this is the view seen by someone who is hiding, and we wonder why the person is hiding. If the establishing shot is from a normally impossible angle, such as from a high corner in a room or looking in a second-story window in a house, we may get the impression that we are invisible observers. Most of the early motion pictures took this point of view, and the better directors established the invisibility of the audience with some such establishing shot. It was something of a shock to audiences in the 1940s when the motion picture *Lady in the Lake* gave the camera a participant's view. Now, however, the technique is used frequently and almost without notice.

Camera mounting with floral clay is simple and effective. Note the safety strap in this case attached to the convenient antenna. Some form of safety strapping is needed in all such setups.

Bicycle-wheel-mounted camera can be steered while in use and can be very effective for running shots with animals or people.

Director and cameraman have to work closely together to get the maximum effectiveness from the script, set, props, and talent.

Modern audiences are well trained visually, and when you produce shows for them you have to speak their visual language. If you violate what they are used to seeing, it had better be for a good reason and one that becomes apparent quickly, or the opportunity will be lost. The camera view itself becomes apparent in the show, so you must be aware of this view as you produce the picture.

FILM AND LIGHTING

Most audiovisual work of an educational or industrial nature, and even a large portion of entertainment audiovisual work, calls for a fairly strict representation of reality. In many cases this dictates that you use an ordinary set of materials and use them in an ordinary way. The job calls for the most realistic images and sequences you can make with camera and film. This usually means having a high budget and a lot of lighting equipment when doing interiors. You will find it almost impossible to get many locations and may have to resort to studio work even in the case in which the client has the location. The client may not want the disturbance in his office, store, or place of business. In the filmstrip business, and I know others who have done it in motion-picture work, I've been able to solve this problem with a chemical solution. If you push Kodak Ektachrome film, or Kodak color negative film in motion pictures, to a speed of ASA 1000 or 1200, you can shoot most store and office interiors and use only a small camera-mounted flash or fill light. In either case the camera-mounted light must be a diffuse source. In still work the Vivitar 283 flash with the diffuser card and holder is ideal. In motion-picture work a Lowell Light with a diffuser may be attached to the camera, or better, the light may be handled by an assistant with a good eye for washing out shadows.

Push processing is generally available at motion-picture labs, but you may have some trouble getting the high-speed Ektachrome film processed at such high indices. If that is the case buy a Unichrome kit and do it yourself. It really is simple, and any photographer who has managed to make a few black-and-white prints can pull it off. In color film processing in small batches, the chemicals should be mixed just before use. Don't mix the entire contents of the kit unless you are going to process that number of rolls of film. The solutions should be used once and thrown out. The only exception to this is if you are going to process the second set immediately and have experimented to determine how much more the first developer should be used to keep the same exposure index.

The first developer is the only critical step in the entire process. This solution must be exactly the correct temperature, and that temperature must be maintained throughout the solution's working period. In the case of push processing, the first developer will be used for 50 to 70 percent more time, typically 13 minutes, and it must be kept in a water bath unless the background temperature is the temperature needed. Agitation every few minutes will do, and the developing tank should be rapped on a hard surface each time the tank is turned over to prevent air bubbles from sticking to the surface of the film.

All of the remaining solutions in the color process can be used at almost any convenient temperature and for any time greater than the kit recommends but never less. The times quoted in the instructions will be minimums, and you will not do any harm by leaving the film in the solutions for longer periods of time.

Pushing the film speed will permit you to shoot in most locations without stacks of stands, lights, and cables running every which way. It is true, however, that your final product will have more grain than a print from film that was not pushed. The grain may not be objectionable to the client if pushing the film has saved the extra time and expense of setting up additional lighting equipment.

To properly use camera and film, you should understand vision and how we see reality. As much as we know about the process of vision, we still don't know how it works internally; most of what we say about the workings of vision is still hypothetical. But, at this time there is enough information and experience available for you to work with camera and film guided by the experience of seeing.

9

Working with People and Animals

Direction is a skill that I believe is almost impossible to teach in a way that will work across the fields of audiovisual production. The difficulty comes from the wide range of material that has to be handled and the many skills needed simultaneously. And, it certainly doesn't help that there is seldom enough money for a project to be properly done, and when there is plenty of money, it seems that all the better people are booked into next year. But, don't despair, because there are some simple principles that you can use to prevent problems before they happen and to stop you from adding to the difficulties.

CHOOSING THE TALENT

The first principle in working with a person or animal is "There is a being in there. Talk to it." So many of us in this business come from the technical side of the enterprise that we tend to focus on the equipment and not the people. In addition, the attractive woman or handsome man who becomes the model or actress or actor is often quite fragile because attractiveness sets her or him apart, and people may be afraid to talk to the person. Isolation can do bad things to people, and you can overcome a lot of potential problems by simply talking with the actress, actor, or model.

The one characteristic that you must insist on in an actor, actress, or model is intelligence. While you cannot give the person an IQ test at the time of the interview, it is possible to gain a feeling for intellect by, again, talking with the person. I have been fooled a couple of times by people who have developed glib interview techniques, but innate intelligence is usually something that shows.

In order to reduce the barriers and have the highest likelihood of

Caroline Leonetti is one of the larger modeling schools and talent agencies in Hollywood. A single phone call to these kinds of services will quickly yield a wide collection of potential models, actors, and actresses.

having a conversation with my potential models and actors and actresses, I never interview in a formal situation. The best place for me to interview is out in the studio at the time the set is being painted. I generally save the painting for last because I want it to be fresh, and generally I also pick up my talent at the last possible minute. When I first started in this business, it seemed a good idea to get just the right face early in the preproduction stage, and because of the nature of my material these faces were generally quite young. On one such occasion a boy whom I had cast several weeks before showed up on the day we were going to shoot with an incredible sunburn. This was the first time I lost my temper on a production, but it certainly was not the last. Now, I cast the models, actresses, and actors the shortest possible time before the shooting sessions, and they are given strict instructions about staying out of the sun, off skateboards, and away from other dangerous activities.

By interviewing in the studio I can see how the potential actress, actor or model will look in the set and how the person will react to light and perhaps other people who will be involved. Interviewing in that kind of location puts the production on a *work* basis from the beginning. There is no fancy puff, hype, or baloney within the bare walls of a barn-like photographic factory—and a factory is all it can be called. How anyone ever got the idea that there is anything glamorous about actually working in this business is beyond me. It is just a lot of hard, often hot, work.

The models, actors, and actresses with whom you will be talking in a studio setting will generally be professionals. If you have any choice in the matter, always go for the professional, and hopefully, trained talent. They will generally give you a better performance, lower production cost, and no surprises. I have seen a few professionals get a slight case of nerves, but I have never seen any professional collapse or be unable to do something needed during a production. Narrators are a special case. Occasionally, a narrator will run into a word that he just cannot say in the way you need it said. One of the first narrators with whom I've ever worked (we must have done 30 shows together) could not say the word *vague* correctly to save his life. In this situation, it is time to grab the script and the pencil and make a substitution rather than waste a lot of tape and studio time. If the script is not your own, be sure you have the right to make a substitution of a synonym, or you can find yourself in a very bad position.

Photographer and two models at the Milan Herzog & Associates studio in Hollywood. Note the umbrellalight-source frame at the left. Two such sources are normally all that are needed to produce the flat light for reproduction

If your production does have dialogue, the actors and/or actresses will have to have the script in sufficient time to have a working knowledge of it, some memorization done, and preferably, some rehearsal time with the director. Most educational and industrial material has very little or no dialogue, and the bulk of a spoken track will be handled by a narrator. The narrator should have the script well in advance of the recording session, as he will want to break the script down in his own way. It does not matter that there are going to be script changes at the last minute. The more the narrator knows about the material, the better he will feel about the session.

As a general rule, I never work with nonprofessional narrators, even for small parts. In some cases, especially when producing training or even selling filmstrips for small companies, the owner, usually the president of the company, will want to do his own narration. I always try to talk him out of it, but if he insists then I insist on one thing: doing it in a professional recording studio. This alone usually scares him out of it because of a great fantasy of super-complicated equipment and large crews who will laugh at him if he goofs. Under no circumstances should you attempt to make a location recording for a selling program. You may be able to get away with it in a sales training program, but the result will only be "getting away with it" and not anything you will want to show anyone in the future. Don't be afraid to tell your client that he shouldn't narrate his own program. He usually will be smart enough to listen to good advice firmly, and privately, given. If he is buying your service and likes your product, he should realize that he is going to have to do some listening. Let him pick the voice for narration from a selection of two or three, but never more than four, voices.

In still photography and some motion-picture situations—ones with nonspeaking parts—you can use a nonprofessional talent if the people are intelligent and understand what they are doing. In the production of a set of filmstrips for the Doubleday Multimedia Company, a subsidiary the parent company closed soon thereafter, we used junior-high-school models with no previous professional experience. However, they were all enrolled in the school's dramatics class. In addition, some of them had taken dancing lessons, and I've found that people with this kind of experience generally move more smoothly and look more natural when photographed in motion. You have to be very careful with boys at the junior-high age, as they can get into visibly awkward positions—their feet seem to point in odd directions and they are very hard on props. You also have to be sure to inspect students' hands before you hire any of them. In this day and age many adolescents are chronic nail biters.

When working with minors you must have the permission of the children's parents, and it is always a good idea to invite the parents along to watch the job. I have never had a parent show up, other than to bring a boy or girl to the studio, and stay for more than a few minutes. I can only attribute this to the fact that the kids probably insisted on being left alone, and the parents complied after having met the photographer. If it is at all possible, I try to do one little shot at the young person's home so the parents can see what is involved. The kids usually go along with this, knowing that you are helping them reassure their parents. In working with young people and their parents, I have always been impressed that the parents were concerned but incredibly well restrained. The parents are always flattered that someone professional wants to photograph their offspring, and they'll usually want outtakes or some clip, still, or whatever. I always plan to give a few stills to the parents when photographing a young model, pro or nonpro.

Relaxing models is a skill that takes time to learn and use. In some cases something silly, like having them jump up and down for a few minutes, will do it, but some people don't like to jump. A lot of conversation and explanation of what you're doing will help in most cases, and if you are working with a complicated setup in which the camera is on a tripod or dolly, it seems to help if the *model* looks through the viewfinder while *you* take his or her place. In my own experience, fear is a product of greeting an unknown. Models and actors and actresses are always at their best when they know what's going on and when things are rolling.

THE LEGALITIES OF AUDIOVISUAL PRODUCTION

In all cases in which you are being paid for the production, you must have a release from a model. I have been casual about this in the past and had no problem, but I have heard of producers who have had people sue them for unauthorized use. It is almost impossible to defend yourself against such a legal action. All the person needs is one print, and if you don't have the release it's all over. Also, if you don't have the right lawyer, and believe me there are wrong ones, you can get sucked into an expensive defense and lose anyway. However, if a person has worked as a professional model or actor or actress and you have a cancelled check plainly labeled "talent fee" or "model fee" for the time period in which the picture or sequence was produced, that is sufficient to prevent you from getting really burned in most courts. However, a judge would have to decide the issue, and this can be expensive and treacherous. I have been on both sides of the fence several times, and I've never been able totally to predict the outcome in court.

Purchasing production insurance, generally for liability alone, is no guarantee that you are going to stay out of trouble. In many ways insurance contracts are not helpful because the insurance company itself is not liable if you are negligent, and you are not likely to get into trouble unless you are negligent in some way. Even in the case in which an accident that could not be prevented happens, the insurance company will often deny payment of the claim. The fact that you have insurance may invite litigation because the injured party may feel that the insurance company has a lot of money. But the party will sue you first, and then you have to sue the insurance company. With the crowded conditions in civil courts now, the whole matter can hang for five years while the attorneys for both sides nibble away at the clients, hitting them for a few hundred dollars here and there. To date I have won every lawsuit in which I've been involved, but don't feel that any of them were worth it. The time involved was an utter waste and could have been much better spent doing *anything* else.

The only way to prevent accidents in production is to plan and plan and plan. Think safety all the time and don't take any chances. Some readers who are familiar with our ski action photography and underwater work will think that statement incredible coming from me, but I have never had a serious accident in a production. The worst thing that has ever happened to me was the second-degree burning of a couple of fingers when I grabbed a hot light fixture. It hurt for a moment, I continued, and only at the end of the day did I find it necessary to apply a bandage. Now that we don't have to use such hot lighting equipment on locations, the safety of production has increased. In addition, camera and metering systems are more reliable than ever, and this has increased the safety factor of productions by letting crews concentrate on safety instead of being distracted by unreliable equipment. Nonetheless, a totally safe production is one that has been planned and planned and planned.

WORKING WITH ANIMALS

Planning is difficult when you are working with animals. Even dogs, quite correctly called our best friends, can be unpredictable when they find several people looking at them and yelling a series of commands. In professional motion-picture productions in which animals are used, the animal trainer is the boss when the animal's segment is filmed. Working with animal actors is always tedious, expensive, and frustrating. Budgets have to be multiplied when animals are written into the scripts, and if people are to be seen on camera with the animals, expensive insurance and elaborate safety precautions have to be taken. Hollywood is full of stories of animals that had been working with models and actors and actresses, had a history of being totally docile, and suddenly viciously turned on the talent. I have worked with domestic and wild animals in farm, zoo, and natural settings, but only rarely have I involved talent with anything other than a dog, cat, or bird. And, in almost all cases it has been the talent's own animal. This is the one way in which I know to guarantee a no-lawsuit production involving an animal, and you usually get better pictures because the owner knows his or her beast and can relate to it.

Wild animals usually call for a lot of stalking or sitting in a blind for hours on end. These are two of the most boring jobs in photography, and they require special people. I've done some of it, but I never look for this kind of work and usually get trapped into it. Still, on those occasions where I have worked with wild animals, I've come away enriched by the experience. Nowhere is this more true than underwater. Whereas you are lucky to get within 6 or 9 m (20 or 30 ft) of land animals, it is possible to approach underwater species virtually to within touching distance. I suppose that the fact that water is 800 times as dense as air and everything appears to be slowed by the water reduces the distance at which the animals take flight, or it may be that their ease of escape gives them confidence. The underwater world is a far different place from land, more like some other planet than a part of the earth. From my experience, photography underwater is the most difficult type of photography, the results are often unpredictable in spite of my own years of experience and a lot of careful planning.

Photography in most strange environments dealing with animals and extreme conditions is usually quite ordinary, but getting there and being effective in these wild locations is the problem. To perform well in the mountains or underwater you must train and prepare for years. It is a matter of staying in excellent physical condition and maintaining your equipment and techniques to guarantee results. If you have to work with federal and state park people to get the locations you need for certain wild animals, be sure you've done your homework, know the behavior patterns of the species, and can work independently. Park people will try to work with you, but their first responsibility is to the animals. As a general rule, any project involving wild animals to be photographed in their natural habitats should have an 18- to 24-month lead time. It will take you that long to find what you want, make all the arrangements to be there at the right time, and let Mother Nature create the right conditions.

In audiovisual production you will have to work with many actors, actresses, models, and animals. There is only one way to go about this and that is with great thoroughness.

10

Art

Most producers of films and filmstrip materials visibly wince when the question of art comes up for discussion. Not only is art expensive, but it is often not as good a use of the medium as are photographs. The formula for creating an effective cartoon character must be one of the great secrets of the universe because it is so seldom accomplished. The worst of these characters strain to be funny or cute, embarrassing the audience while doing violence to the material and the producer's budget. In several cases in which I've seen really abominable cartoon characters in film programs and asked the producers about them, the explanation has been the same. They left the creation of the character up to the artist because they felt this person should know what to do, and by the time the drawings were done, they had spent so much money that it was impossible to change. This is gross mismanagement, but I've seen otherwise good producers do it time after time.

Don't ever be snowed by an artist. The good artists are usually high priced, but they are worth it. You can either afford the best original art or you can't afford any of it. The exception to this rule is the young person just out of school who has a genuine innate ability. If you can, find this artist before anyone else and hire him or her for his or her first job. This event will happen once or twice in a lifetime of producing. The only way to choose an artist is to see some pencil tests and pick an approach that you like. When a character is right, it jumps off the page, whether it is in pencil or in color. Never accept the line "It'll improve with color." When the character is right, you will know it.

(Above) Headquarters for the MCB
Corporation in a dawn establishing
shot. Narration: "Another day is about
to begin at MCB; let's go in and see how
it works." (Right) An interior shot made
for a Universal Education and Visual
Arts production called Let's Vote shows
a Los Angeles City Councilman and a
young male model ostensibly discussing
a project.

DISCOVERING NATURE SERIES

For this series on discovering nature, a juvenile model was photographed from a very low angle with a 14 mm lens.

The bee in the flower was chilled in a refrigerator to reduce its activity.

TV COMMERCIAL SERIES

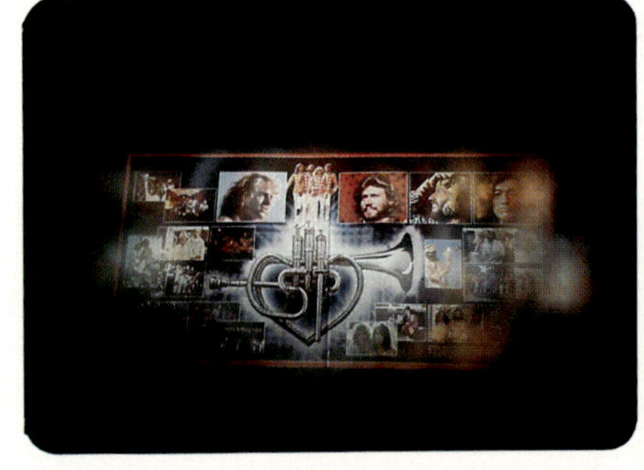

Stills made for a television commercial for the film Sergeant Pepper's Lonely Hearts Club Band, produced by the Robert Stigwood Organization. The stills were converted to videotape for TV broadcasting.

A dead butterfly was mounted on a leaf for this shot, taken with a normal lens.

The young male model was photographed out of focus for scale representation behind a snail.

SKI SERIES

A 12 mm fisheye lens was used for this shot at the top of Mammoth Mountain, California, at the entrance to The Cornice.

Example of a camera mounted on a ski, jumping a low mogul (bump).

A young model in eighteenth-century costume and set. Note the relative simplicity of the period set.

Shot taken by a ski-mounted camera, at moderate speed during a left turn on an open slope. Fill flash by an electronic flash mounted on the camera illuminated the flying snow.

A grab shot made with a Nikonos used as a ski-action camera, taken from a chair lift. An aperture of f/22 produced the sun "star" effect; shutter speed was either 1/250 or 1/500 sec.

A shot from Candle 1790 *on the use of candlelight in the late eighteenth century.*

This special effect shot was made using a "5C" Spiratone accessory lens.

A young model in a show called Using the Metric System *produced for Universal Education and Visual Arts.*

A posterized shot of drummer-singer Levon Helm demonstrates the considerable effectiveness of this technique, especially when used with an image having a wide range of densities.

This effect was achieved on a flat art collage by using a "Center Sharp" Spiratone lens.

The author using a telescope for the filmstrip series You in the Universe.

CEL ART

All figures and paintings for films or filmstrips should be done in what is called *twelve field*. This is a drawing field that is 22.9 × 30.5 cm (9" × 12") and is usually ruled on a 27.9 × 35.6 cm (11" × 14") piece of posterboard or animation *cel*. The term *cel* comes from the word celluloid, the material from which these transparent drawing sheets originally were made. Now they are made from 5/1000-inch-thick acetate plastic; the drawings are done on one side, the reverse side of the way in which they will be seen, and color is applied to the other side. The result is an extremely fine, saturated color image of the highest quality that can be had for film work. Of course this quality comes at a price, and it is often higher than needed for this work. The big benefit in having cels made, in addition to the color quality, is the fact that they can be moved from one background to another. This gives you several drawings for the price of one, and if your writing and planning are very carefully done, you can actually save money by using cels.

The backgrounds for cel art are often painted by air brush, which is a small pneumatic spray gun of great precision—so much precision that the gun can be used as a brush. Air-brushing equipment is expensive, and the technique of using it is special. This is a great tool in the hands of a qualified artist and a treacherous toy in the hands of an artist not properly trained. Again, be sure you see some examples of the artist's work before you commission anything to be done by air brush.

If the color paintings you need are only going to be used once, the expense of cels is not justified. The thought that you *may* be able to use the cels in the future is probably not justified either, and I've only been able to do it on a few occasions. Drawings of medical subjects and biological specimens are the best candidates for subsequent use. Few other drawings will have future value for most producers because there is always some little change or alteration needed, and cels are impossible to modify. They are also difficult to store because the acetate surface is very soft and easily scratched. If you are planning to use cel art, plan to use it once.

BURN-IN ART

Most art that is needed for the current style of production is little more than title art or other burn-in material. My favorite of all the systems to make these white letters on a black background is the system using Kodalith film and hand-applied letters, which can be purchased in art supply stores. These letters are printed on the backs of plastic sheets. When you place the

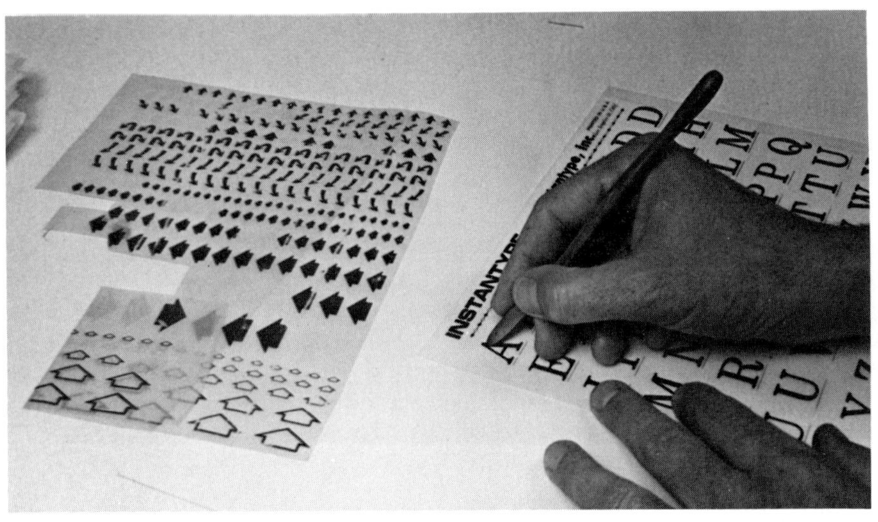

Instant-Type can be applied with a wooden embosser to any paper or poster-board surface. These letters are very quick to use and can be converted to white letters with Kodalith negative film.

letter on the posterboard or paper to which it is to be applied, rub the plastic side with a special burnishing tool, and the letter soon sticks to the paper surface. With a little planning it is possible to produce very effective titles, labels, and captions in black letters on a white surface. The original art is then photographed using Kodalith film, which is then processed in its own special high-contrast developer. Unlike continuous-tone film systems, this material records everything in either black or white. It has extremely high resolution and makes the clearest, sharpest letters in the whitest white on the blackest black. The other systems of hot press and cold press, used to put plastic white letters on acetate cel material which is then photographed over a black background, do not give as sharp or clear an image. However, the one advantage these plastic letters have over the Kodalith burn-ins is that they can be used in aerial-image work where an art or photographic background is projected and made visible by a large *field lens*. A field lens is as large as the field to be viewed and these huge, long-focal-length magnifying glasses are usually 11″ × 14″. A 22.9 × 30.5 cm (9″ × 12″) field is used, and cel art or titles are placed in front of the lens.

When the art or photograph to be copied is projected in such an aerial-image system, and the art or title to be copied is placed on the field, the illumination can be varied to balance the exposure, giving a perfect copy the first time. This is the process used for making mixtures of live action and animated characters. It is a tedious process, incredibly expensive but effective. The aerial-image process is seldom used for anything but big-budget children's films, almost the exclusive domain of the Disney corporation, and a few breakfast food commercials, where money doesn't matter when it comes to convincing little kids of the merits of Sugar Pops. For a short time the process was used for handling titles in filmstrips, but the expense soon put it out of business in this area. Today most titles are done as Kodalith burn-ins. The experience needed to make them nearly as effective as aerial-image work is a part of virtually every film lab specializing in filmstrip internegatives.

You can make your own titles and burn-ins with Kodalith film and press-on letters. Art supply stores carry a thin kind of posterboard called *railroad board,* and after you purchase several 55.9 × 71.1 cm (22" × 28") sheets, they will be glad to cut it into 27.9 × 35.6 cm (11" × 14") panels, four to the sheet. This is marvelous material with which to work. It has a hard, permanent surface that will take a lot of erasing if you sketch on it lightly. However, if you are going to ink it, the amount of erasing is critical. The moment the surface becomes abraded or roughened in any way, the ink will begin to run on it. In some cases in which I did want to make an ink master on a surface on which I knew there had been too many erasures, I placed a piece of 22.9 × 30.5 cm (9" × 12") tracing paper over the board, did the ink drawing, and then taped it to a clean posterboard for reversal photography or the next step of the process.

If I am beginning to sound like an experienced artist to you, the impression is incorrect. I know very little about art but dabble in it continually. Some of this dabbling has been done out of necessity, some for convenience, and much for the creative potential it holds. One of the great delights of the audiovisual business is that it permits, if not requires, you to play in all these various fields. Most of the images used in this business are only on the screen for a short time, often just a few seconds, and it is amazing how simple they have to be to work well. The simplest few lines of a drawing executed well and with taste are more effective than a great piece of art painstakingly drawn. The only exception to this is the large master drawing or painting, done on 76 × 102 cm (30" × 40") posterboard or on masonite, that is toured by the camera, getting many frames of filmstrip or many seconds of motion picture or video. For most educational and industrial films and filmstrips the simple image works best.

THE ROTOSCOPE

One of the best tools for the inexperienced artist or chronic dabbler is called a *rotoscope.* Regardless of whatever mirrors and accessory lenses are used to bring the image into focus, the rotoscope is simply a slide projector focused on a small, usually 22.9 × 30.5 cm (9″ × 12″) field. When converting from a slide to a filmstrip, motion-picture, or video format, you have to give up a portion of the image on either side. This is due to the fact that the 35 mm slide format is 24 × 36 mm, or 1:1.5, and the filmstrip, motion-picture, and video formats are, or are very close to, 18 × 24 mm or 1:1.33. An occasional image gives some difficulty in this conversion, but most photographers shoot with enough margin to allow the conversion to happen naturally.

The rotoscope allows you to place titles in dark areas where they will virtually leap off the screen. It permits you to place labels where they belong, include arrows and outlines in the visuals, and do other tricks that look like magic on the screen. Whatever you place with the rotoscope goes down in the form of a black letter or line. It is then photographed on Kodalith film and copied in the internegative at the same time the first visual goes onto the film stock. After some experience with the rotoscope, you may want to try to do the process without the slide projection equipment by projecting the image mentally. This can be done by putting the background slide in a slide viewer and holding it in your left hand while looking at the slide through your left eye and looking at the posterboard with your right eye. The limits of the 22.9 × 30.5 cm field should be lightly penciled onto the card, and the

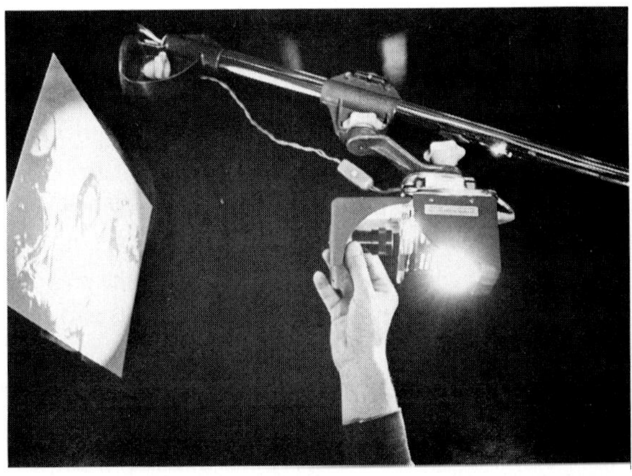

Rotoscope projection can be accomplished with a small slide projector and short focal length lens. Most enlargers will not carry a mounted slide or give sufficient illumination.

slide can then be "projected" so its upper and lower limits fit those on the card. This process works well if the title or burn-in to be placed does not require a great deal of accuracy. The flexibility of the process can be improved if the title is first set on paper strips so it can be moved around as you simultaneously look through the slide viewer and at the card. You have to be very quick and decisive for this process to work well because slide viewers require the eye to be at infinity focus, the relaxed position for the eye's lens, and your viewing distance for the penciled-in area on the card will probably be something like 61 cm (2 ft). Both eyes focus together, an unfortunate fact of our present development and one which evolution will hopefully correct, and you will have to continually switch back and forth from slide to card as you make your decision.

There are so many new artists' aids now on the market and soon to be on the market that it helps to become familiar with these things in the art supply stores. The sales personnel in these stores are often knowledgeable, and if you explain your problem to them, they will often come up with a solution. The same people who make the press-on letters that you can use for titles also make arrows, lines, caligraphic patterns, geometric patterns, and even cartoon figures. All of these patterns are in the public domain, and you can use them in any kind of program without restriction. The only thing you cannot do with these figures is copy them in some way in which you would in turn sell them as press-on figures.

USING COPYRIGHTED ART

The issue of copyright applicability and ownership is one that is very complicated and often hard to determine. If you are making a show for your own use or strictly to demonstrate your own talents, you can use anything. If you find an illustration in a book still under copyright protection, it will be necessary to contact the publisher and work out some kind of licensing arrangement. These agreements are usually very simple, often no more than a single letter wherein the owner of the copyright, either the author or the publisher, grants you the permission to use the image for a particular show, with or without restrictions. The larger publishers have their own divisions of rights and permissions usually run by a staff of attorneys who can make this process as simple or as complicated as they wish. The smaller publishers generally leave the copyright in the author's name, and you will have to deal with the author or artist directly. Most of these people are easy to do business with; they are glad to have the extra exposure and money. If you are told you can have a figure drawn for $25 to $50 using the original as a model, the artist who owns the original image will usually be glad for a $10 or $15 use fee.

In a recent production I found a large periodic table that I liked very much and wanted to use, so I wrote to the publisher, who was also the artist. The letter came back stamped with the legend that it could not be delivered because the party was no longer at that address and there was no forwarding address. I repeated the procedure, saving the original letter, and the same thing happened a second time. I then used the chart in the show, and I am still prepared to pay the artist a reasonable use fee, but he apparently has vanished. Some producers would not take this chance, and they have a point if I am going to recommend the path of greatest caution and least hazard. However, issues such as these are settled on what the courts call "industry-wide practice," and for the kind of show I produced using this chart—an educational filmstrip—there is no way I could be asked to pay more than $50 for its use. Thus, no attorney would take a case of this kind for an out-of-state publisher who would lose in winning a $50 settlement. Also, I will be glad to pay the artist if he ever sends me a letter; his chart is excellent and it helped my show.

STOCK IMAGE HOUSES

There are many stock image houses that deal in material for film, filmstrip, magazine, and book publishers. Most of these places are careful to deal in public-domain material, but if they should mistakenly sell you something that is under copyright protection, you will still have a liability problem. Bettmann Archive Inc., 136 East 57th St., New York, NY, is probably the best known of the stock image houses. I have never been able to get together with them because their prices are very high. However, I've been able to find adequate illustrations in local libraries and old-book stores. Old-book store owners are a very special class of people. Most of them know, to an amazing degree, what they have in the midst of huge heaps of crusty, dusty material. However, I've done some extensive digging and discovered things that no one knew were there. Another excellent source of public-domain illustrations is the Dover Publication Company, 180 Varick St., New York, NY 10014. Many of their volumes include the declaration that up to 10 images may be used in any one project without charge. I have written to them periodically for others of their books, and they have given me permission with no charge every time. Nonetheless, I still recommend writing to them concerning *your* project because I just may have asked for material that is in the public domain.

COPYRIGHT LAW

The issue of copyright and what it means is a ball that has been and will be bouncing for a very long time. Certainly the artist deserves protection, and it is in the public interest to see that the artist is protected. If we don't protect our sources, there eventually will be no sources. This is the mechanism that killed the overhead-transparency business. When this process was developed, it was correctly hailed as a great boon to the truly creative teachers. It permitted them to simultaneously project a full-color image, make additions to it, point to it, and yet maintain eye contact with the class because the image was projected over the teacher's shoulder by a first-surface mirror. The educational publishers immediately jumped into this business, producing elaborate and expensive 21.6 × 27.9 cm (8½" × 11") transparencies, thousands of them, on every phase of every subject. But the 3M Company then came along with a process and machine that permitted the schools to make full-color copies of any of these professionally produced transparencies. Boom—the bottom dropped out of the business. The schools would buy one and make hundreds of duplicates. Whereas the educational publishers had every right to expect a market of hundreds of thousands of each transparency over the years, it soon became apparent that the market would be only hundreds, and each transparency would sell only once because the schools would keep the original on file and duplicate it.

This same thing can happen with motion pictures in education if video taping is allowed to happen without restriction. I don't think that this will ruin the educational motion-picture business, because the large companies cannot afford to let it happen. They wrote off the transparency business because it was still small and the infringements were happening everywhere. In addition, the infringements were being done with equipment that had a proper application in the school and was used to make original materials. The process for stealing an educational motion picture is one that requires specific, expensive equipment set up by someone who knows what he is doing and who could become subject to criminal, as well as civil, penalties. The principle of copyright is violated in both cases, but the potential for severe prosecution would only seem to be found in the educational motion-picture field.

It is generally not known how easily copyright can be obtained by anyone. While the law states that the Copyright Office in Washington, D.C. requires two copies of the work, a filled out form registering the work in the correct class, and a fee of $10, the fact of the matter is that all you have to do is put "© 19__ by *(your name)*" on the picture, script or whatever you want protected. In the case in which there is an infringement, you still have to prosecute the case, and the fact that you don't have the certificate doesn't matter because courts have consistently held that the fact that you did not file the form does not mean you had no intention of doing so. Also, the person or persons who infringed on the copyright did break the law. This is a most convenient situation for writers and artists of all types because it means that for the price of a new rubber stamp every year you can protect every picture, article, or whatever to the limits of the law.

Artwork should not be complicated or expensive for audiovisual productions. There are so many new materials and techniques for making and using art that this phase of the production, which used to be universally feared by producers watching budgets, can now be approached casually. The small producer should become involved in this phase of the production because the more he knows of his medium, the better he will be able to produce in it. The next chapter explores the utilization of art and photographic materials in the relatively new field of special effects. This is probably one of the most exciting fields in audiovisual production, and it is one that permits you to obtain better, more expensive artwork by permitting you to utilize it in a broader fashion in your show.

11

Special Effects

When good photography is not enough, special effects are in order. But, knowing how to make odd visual images in such situations is not sufficient. There are guiding principles in this work, and while they are obvious, it is apparent that many photographers and program producers don't keep them in mind. The first guiding principle of special-effects work extends directly from the objective: There must be a single point to be made in any one visual image unless it is a transition frame or sequence. A confusion of images is just that, a confusion, and something meaningful had better come out of it before too many seconds pass.

All special-effects work is part of a sequence. If the image or scene is dark, then the subsequent special effect will also have to be dark, or it will interrupt the flow of the program. There are points where you do want punctuation or an abrupt change of direction. This is the time when you will want to abruptly change the light intensity of the screen. Nonetheless, the general flow of your sequence can be better maintained if you stay at one level of brightness and on one side of the spectrum. If you are working with strong blue images, you may want to flow across the spectrum through the greens, yellows, oranges, and reds, but not change quickly from an essentially blue scene to a red one. At this time the colors seen in most professional cinematography are muted and soft, tending to flow rather easily from one scene to the next. It will probably be a very long time before we again see the stunning brilliance of the Technicolor world of Oz. The color softness that is now seen on the screen simplifies sequence planning.

In most special-effects work reality is distorted. The one exception to this is photomicrographic work; it is often grouped with camera and film tricks, but it is better described as an unusual view rather than a special one. Most special-effects images are altered representations of reality. As you work with these systems, make the images, and use them on audiences, you will begin to appreciate how much perception is projection. In large measure people see what they expect to see because the information on which they base their perception is incomplete. The eye sees well only in a very narrow path, two degrees (the width of a 12× telephoto lens field), and as a result we have a highly focused intellect. We see and think about one thing at a time in spite of the fact that many things are continually happening around us. In the room where you now read this page, there are many items that you have seen recently and cataloged in your mind. Let me add to that inventory a large clock that ticks slowly. You have not seen it, but you know it is there because you can hear it. Its sound is of a type that you know only comes from a large Seth Thomas mantle clock, and in your mind you can see it. Your projection of this clock is just as real as would be your recollection of it had it been there. You can convince audiences of such realities with sound and photographic effects. Sound effects are a special issue in themselves, and

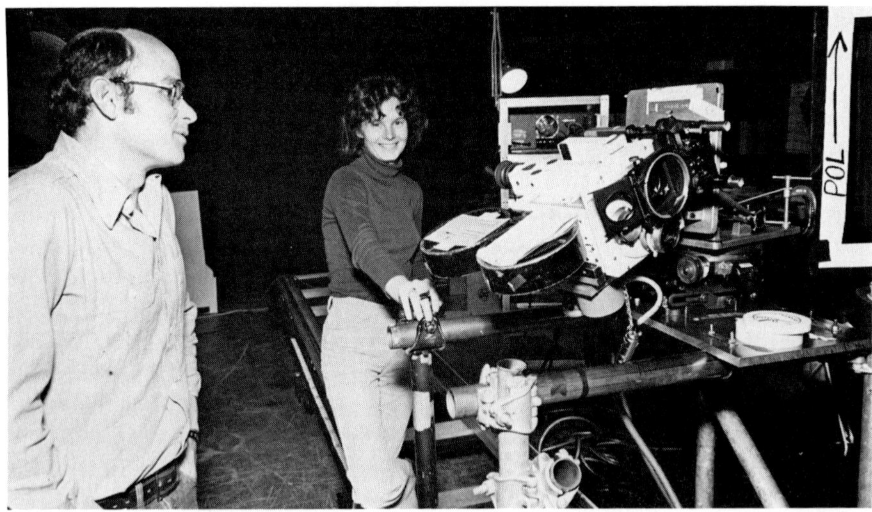

Cameraman Jim Villeaux and assistant Diana Wooten discuss an upcoming shot with a computer-animated camera system at the Filmation Studio in Hollywood, California.

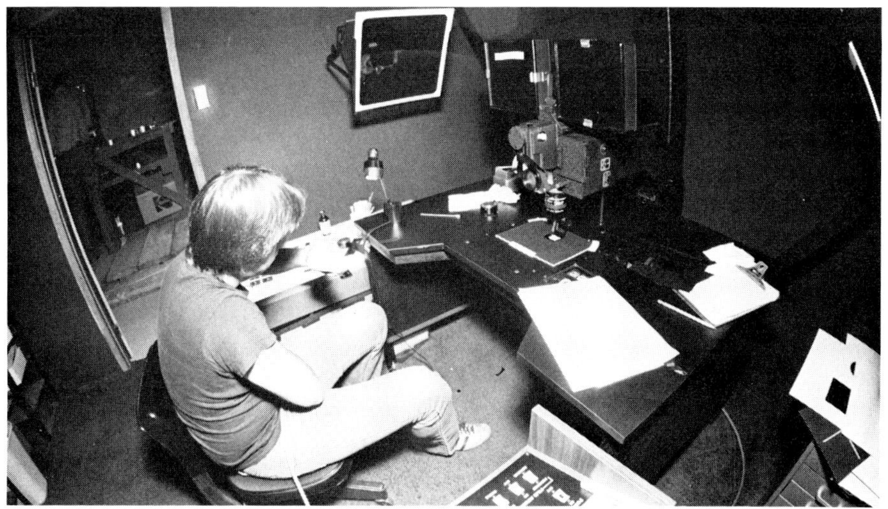

The Image Stream precision camera system for making special-effects images for multi-image shows is operated by Ted Iserman of the organization.

one that will be covered in the next chapter, but photographic effects can be even stronger in projecting a "You Are There" experience.

One of the hottest new media in the audiovisual business today is the multi-screen, multi-projector show operated by a programmed cueing tape or memory. Several of these shows now have the names "The New York Experience," "The San Francisco Experience," and so on. The name is significant because it is so accurate in describing the feeling you have after seeing one of these shows. You've been there. Of course, the thing is a teaser for the host city's tourist industry and a very effective one where it is used. The important point for us is that these shows work because human beings are adapted to function with incomplete information. The utter reality of a motion-picture or slide show of this advanced kind is possible because we internalize so little of what is going on around us. Thus, give the audience a fleeting glance of what you want them to see, be sure they can hear it in the background, and for them it will be there.

There are two general areas of special-effects work dealing directly with camera and film; one deals with camera implements and the other with techniques. There is yet a third area, but this has nothing to do with either camera or film and can best be described as conjuring or magic. In essence, this is the art of creating a visual illusion with special suspension-systems mirrors, painted rods, and colored backgrounds to make things appear to levitate and perform other magic. In Hollywood when you say "special-effects," it is the kind of work which generally comes to mind. Most of it is very mechanical, certainly not magical, fairly boring, and frustrating for the people involved. It comes off on the screen only because most of what was really happening is not seen, and weeks of work will flash by in minutes. In most audiovisual production you do not have to go to the trouble of having a Hollywood motion-picture company to get what you need. For slide shows, filmstrips, and even video applications, the tricks can be simpler, but still effective.

CAMERA IMPLEMENTS

Lens-like accessories

Most of the camera implements used in special-effects work are of the accessory-lens type, lens-like devices that are attached to the front of a normal or mildly telephoto lens. Wide-angle lenses do not usually adapt well to this kind of work because this accessory device often vignettes the field. This effect in itself can be of use, but only in rare dream or recall sequences. One of the most valuable of these kinds of lens-like devices is the soft-focus accessory, which is a lightly sandblasted optical flat cut and mounted in a filter holder. These attachments come in series and millimetre sizes, and you can get them at many camera stores. They are especially good for working with women in soft or dreamy situations. In this same category there is also a center-sharp soft-focus accessory. This is a ground and polished diopter lens, wherein the center circular area, usually one-quarter the diameter of the entire element, is left optically flat. The result is that the outer edges of the frame have a different focus point than the center; the center remains sharp, and the outer edges go soft in a halo fashion. This latter accessory is my favorite of its type because of the halos and the fact that the center of the field remains sharp. One of the basic principles of this business is that something in the field has to be sharp, and this attachment gives it to you.

The multiple-image accessory attachments are of this same kind, but they are cut from much thicker circles of optical glass. In spite of this, no exposure correction is needed when you use one of these accessories, but there will be an observable focus shift. In all cases, when working with any accessory lens-like device added to the front of the camera, *focus at the f-stop at which the picture will be made.* This will not only ensure that you will see the effect that will be recorded—and the effect does change with a change in the *f*-stop—but it will guarantee that the portion of the image you want to be in focus will be sharp.

Multiple-image accessory lenses are made in two basic varieties—those with several large facets and those with a series of small steps. The first kind breaks the image into three, four, five, or six images, depending on the number of facets, and presents them in much the same geometry as seen on the face of the attachment. There is some overlapping, but you can control this with a change in the *f*-stop. The step lenses, usually having five steps each cut at a slightly steeper angle, produce a repeated image that appears to "step" into space. Two of these used on top of one another can create real confusion in the camera and give you more choices than you'll ever need.

There are now several types of diffraction-grating lens accessories, but the best of them is the Kalt Color-Burst version because it keeps the effect in the field. Most of the diffraction-grating lens accessories allow the spectrum effect to go off to one side of the field and are thus of limited use. The Kalt version has corrected this fault, and it is of great use. The one problem in all of this kind of photography is that you have to be careful to

Special-effects accessory lenses available from Spiratone, Inc. break images into several parts, thus extending the use of art and the making of transition images.

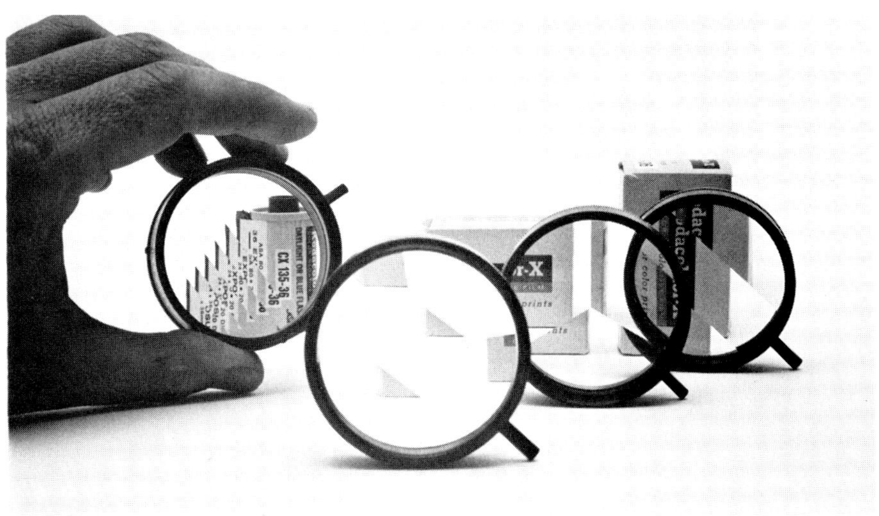

shoot a normal, unaltered reference or stock frame at the time you're doing the special-effects frames. It is easy to get so carried away with all the fantastic effects that you forget that the audience frequently has to see some normal scenes to appreciate the incredible versions. All special-effects photography will be more effective if the audience has some experience with the source material, and this often means seeing a normal version of a scene first.

Perhaps one of the best-known and least well-used accessory lenses is the Weegee device invented by the late Arthur Fellig, a New York street photographer best known for his crime and violence pictures and later this one special-effect device. Weegee, like a lot of "street guys" who made good, had the ability not only to produce work of interest, but to puff it up with "hype" in the days before the expression existed. Sometime in the middle fifties Weegee discovered that a sheet of Plexiglas could be made pliable in an ordinary oven at 135 C (275 F), and if bent in an odd shape, images would be distorted in interesting ways. He made a few pictures with this system, took them to one of the popular photographic magazines, and stunned the

The Weegee lens, mounted on a stand for precise handling, can also be hand-held for some bizarre effects. Made by heating Plexiglas to 135 C (275 F) in an oven, it needs only slight bending and distortion to be effective.

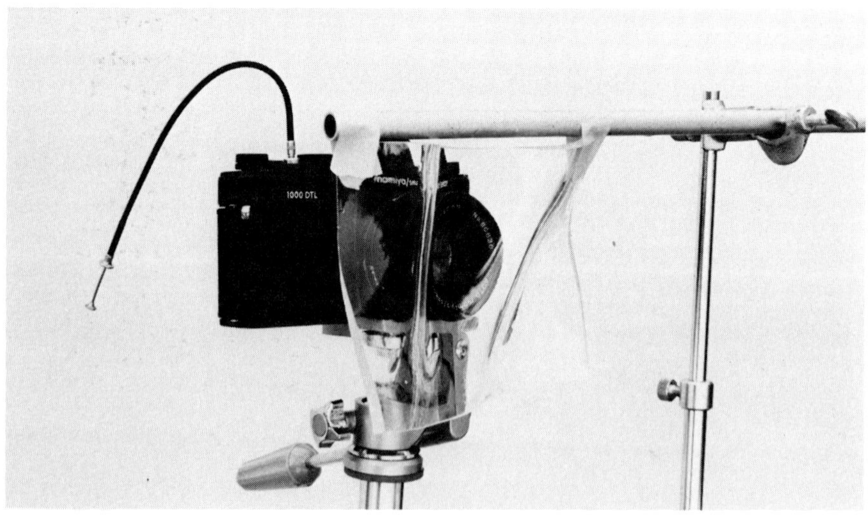

editors. These were the days when the national camera fever was just beginning to catch on. The Japanese manufacturers had virtually conquered the market. Photography and the magazines dealing with photography were hot. An innovation of the kind Weegee had invented could, and did, cause a lot of excitement in the printed media. Furthermore, Weegee kept the system a secret and milked it for every last nickel in all the better picture magazines. He finally revealed the nature of his process, and in true storybook fashion he died shortly thereafter. Unfortunately, most of the Weegee imitators lacked the taste of the originator and ran the system into the ground in short order. I have included the Weegee system in my own bag of tricks, not because it has been particularly effective in my own work, but because the potential is there and I am still hopeful of using it well.

The kaleidoscope system

Another system that I do not use very often, and one that has one glaring technical problem, is the kaleidoscope system. In essence it consists of two long, rectangular mirrors held together in a "V" fashion. At one end of the shallow trough formed by the mirrors, a sample of flat art is placed in contact with the ends of the mirrors. The camera is focused on the juncture of the mirrors, with this point centered, and the lens is operated at its smallest opening. The problem with the system is depth of field. There is some amount of exposure difficulty because the mirrors absorb light in each reflection, and some of the images are of the third order, coming from two reflections. The images are best used quickly so that only an impression of the flower-like image is given; the image should not be held on the screen long enough to be studied in detail. Kaleidoscope images are almost always transition images, used in passing from one distinct sequence to another. They allow you to expand your use of art, but do require careful composition and use.

Starburst filters

Another type of special-effects accessory is called the starburst filter. It is not really a filter because the device is cut from an optical flat that is held in a filter ring, and it normally does not require any exposure correction. You can make various kinds of these devices by cutting blank-filter sized circles from light plastic or clear acetate. The starburst effect comes from light lines ruled on the surface of the plastic with a thin X-acto knife. The first set of lines is ruled in a parallel fashion all the way across the circle. If you put the plastic in a filter holder and focus the camera on a point light source, such as a candle, you will see the effect at this point. It will be a single line radiating

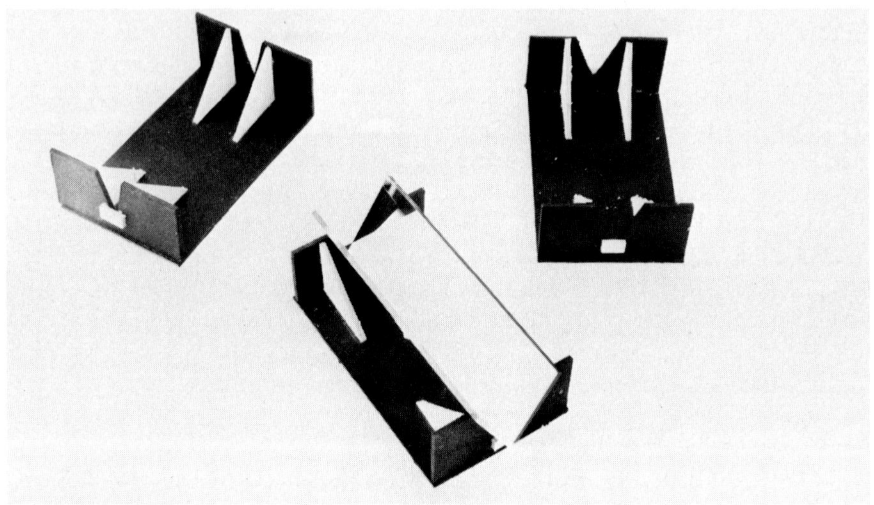

Three kaleidoscope holders made for first-surface mirrors will produce the classic flower-like image in a camera aimed down the long axis of the optical "trough."

from the point source and running perpendicular to the ruled series of lines. If another series of lines is ruled perpendicular to the first series, a second effect of a line perpendicular to the first will be produced. Yet another series of ruled lines at another angle will add another effect, and so on.

There is a practical limit to the number of series of lines you can rule on one plastic circle because each series softens the image due to light interruption and halation. Generally, two sets of rulings are the limit, but in a special application you may want to make more as well as have your own at some angle other than 90 degrees.

The beam splitter and front projection

In this category of camera implements must be included the beam splitter and front projection. A beam splitter allows you to photograph two images simultaneously, and the usual reason for using this is to create some magical effect in motion-picture or video production. In still photography it is usually easier to simply make a double exposure because the simultaneity of the recorded event is guaranteed by the process. The primary difficulty that most photographers have with beam splitters is a geometric one. Contrary to the appearance through the viewfinder, one set of events is taking place 90 degrees away from the other, and this is more than the mind can master in a working situation. The solution is to fix everything to one plane, usually level or horizontal, thus limiting subject motions to back and forth and from one side of the frame to the other. This limit really restricts the work and makes it more of a mechanical exercise than a creative process. As a result, few photographers really enjoy beam-splitter techniques.

Front projection would seem to be the special-effects photographer's nirvana because it permits you to project any slide through a beam splitter through which the camera simultaneously looks. The image of the projected slide must fall on a special screen of high reflectance, and the best type for this purpose is made by the 3M Company. As with most proprietary products sold these days, the price is high. Lenticular screens will work in a front-projection system, but not as well as the 3M product.

My objections to front projection are many in spite of the fact that it is the only practical solution to some photographic problems. Certain effects, like people flying in space, can best be done by this process rather than by getting into tricky matting and screen work that will be just as expensive and not as reliable. Important people or talent with limited time can only be properly photographed by some such trick process if you want to place them in a distant environment or in one that is very special. Quick catalog work with high production values, and prices to match, can best be done by the front-projection system. But, the image on the screen always looks like a postcard background unless it has been carefully prepared for this process. The system is so complicated and demanding that it should have one technician, preferably the person who set it up and works with it often, to run the actual setting up and projection. Lighting ratios are crucial, and a lot of overshooting is necessary. This usually ruins the spontaneity that is now so highly prized by today's clients. The subjects often look stiff and posed because they are stiff and posed due to all the equipment, time for setting up, and photography.

In spite of the fact that it is a technical marvel, I would go to front projection only as a last resort, and only in those cases where there is virtually no other way to get what you need. If you are going to do a lot of this kind of work, it quickly will become apparent that you are better off owning the equipment rather than running to someone else's studio all the time. In addition, there is the creative importance of having a hands-on familiarity with the equipment. This fact is true in all audiovisual work. If you understand these processes and work with them, you will be able to do things that other producers cannot do.

Split Diopter Lenses, First-Surface Mirrors, and Partial Filters

The final items to be mentioned in this section of camera implements include split diopter lenses, first-surface mirrors, and partial filters. These are lumped together in a subsection of what I would call items of lesser interest, simply because they are so seldom used but regularly advertised. The split diopter lens is a close-up lens that has been sawed in half, and it can be used to present a close object and a distant background in simultaneous sharp focus. My objection to this accessory is that there is a distinct borderline between these two areas of focus unless you use the lens near wide open, and if you do, the depth of focus of the foreground subject is so shallow it is almost useless. The number of times that I have actually been able to make one of these lenses work well, or even have seen examples of their good use, is small. Still, they do exist, and it is worth knowing of their potential.

First-surface mirrors of the ordinary kind, usually 7.6 or 10.2 cm by 12.7 or 15.2 cm (3 or 4 in. by 5 or 6 in.) on a side, are rarely useful in special-effects photography. The only usable effect that I've ever produced with one of these mirrors was that of putting a lake in an area where one didn't exist

Suction-cup-mounted, first-surface mirror, used here to make a synthetic
"lake" filling the San Fernando Valley. This type of effect can be stunningly
real when used sparingly.

to enhance the scene. Effects of this kind are what I call "reaching too far" in most cases, and the difficulty of caring for one of these mirrors to keep the delicate "first surface" intact makes it time consuming. Most photographic equipment that is going to be used on location has to be rugged, and these mirrors are, by their very nature, fragile.

The partial filters are of two kinds, and I believe that they are of interest only to amateurs and those producers who do nothing but make multi-screen shows. The one characteristic these two groups have in common is that they normally must project original material. Producers who make filmstrips, motion pictures, printed materials, and so forth have the opportunity to add color effects in the reproduction stage. The partial filter is generally placed in front of the lens at the time the original is shot. This is another case in which you must compose the scene with the lens set at the taking aperture. The filter is moved in front of the lens until the desired effect is seen, and then the picture is made. The filters may be made of glass, as in the commercial versions, or cut from plastic gel materials available from art supply stores. I prefer the latter method because the gels offer a greater range of color at a lower price, and the gels are lighter in weight and dispensable.

Special-effects projection setup featuring a ground glass facing a first-surface mirror. The effect was used extensively in the final sequence of the motion pic-ture 2001: A Space Odyssey.

SPECIAL TECHNIQUES

If we accept that a "normal" photograph is one taken with a lens of a focal length equal to the diagonal of the film, at a shutter speed of 1/60 sec. and a typical outdoor f-stop of $f/16$, then every picture taken with other lenses and at other settings is a special-effects photograph. I think that this idea is very important, and I have selected these figures because the normal lens produces a picture convenient to the regular scanning mode of the eye. A shutter speed of 1/60 sec. will produce a picture that is sharp, not blurred by motion. And, $f/16$ will give a usable depth of field wherein everything will be of acceptable sharpness. This is our home base or starting point in photography, and one to which we will return often. A number of years ago, I made a study of my own work in terms of the focal length and most probable f-stops and shutter settings used. Over 100 filmstrips were sampled, and it was soon apparent that almost everything was being shot with a normal lens at "normal" settings. Of course, educational filmstrip is functional, representational work. The exposition is one of reality, and the target is ignorance, which you don't prevail over by confusing the audience. Still, a similar study of my own more recent work, and this work is for business and entertainment clients, is showing much the same kind of result, and yet I am now referred to as a "special-effects expert."

It is my own conclusion that the reason the fact of my photographic work is different from the legend is that the special-effects work has been done and presented in such a way that it stands out. I've not run it into the ground because I know the importance of operating from and returning to the home base of photography—the normal image. In addition, many of my images are from special places, underwater as well as from high altitudes, and these images often appear to be special-effects work when the photography is ordinary.

Underwater photography

Underwater photography is really never ordinary. The circumstances under which you do the work are normally life threatening, the equipment is awkward to use, the light is of an entirely different and changing nature, the subject matter is totally unlike anything else you will ever photograph, and most importantly, your mind is never really clear. Thinking is apparently such a delicate process that it can be disturbed by a change as subtle as the pressure of air. It is common knowledge that most divers will begin to show the symptoms of nitrogen narcosis at a depth of 27.4 m (90 ft), initially a mild intoxication increasing to a debilitating one at great depths with long exposure. It is not commonly accepted that the mind-altering effects of an

Nikonos underwater cameras, high-speed-film/wide-angle-lens version on the left and normal lens with flash on the right. Note close-up lens with focusing cord for the second unit.

increased quantity of nitrogen begin to happen at shallow depths. I have experienced these effects at 7.6 to 9.1 m (25 to 30 ft), finding three-figure subtraction problems almost impossible to do accurately. This makes underwater navigation very difficult unless you have a predesigned plan to which you adhere. A surface conference with your diving partner will become necessary if there is a change in plans.

Another part of the difficulty of thinking underwater is due to the distraction factor. This means that you must design an underwater photographic system to virtually function by itself, or so simple even an inexperienced person could handle it. Underwater photography is a special field in its own right and, correctly, the subject of several books. If this field is to be one of your specialties, you must set aside a year of Sundays to learn the diving and other special skills needed for underwater photography. At the beginning of your second year in this field, you may be able to come back with professionally acceptable results regularly.

High-altitude photography

High-altitude work is not as demanding as diving, but you should be in very good physical condition and have experience in backpacking, climbing, or skiing, depending on the objective. In all such cases the smallest, lightest system is the best system, and reliability comes from experience, not brand name. I have long heard that Nikon, for example, is the most reliable camera. I have owned and used seven different camera systems in my career and have found that all of them will give you some amount of trouble and in approximately equal quantities. The only way that

I have ever been able to depend on my system was to have two camera
bodies and a fairly regular maintenance program. In today's competitive
marketplace I don't think it is possible to buy a bad camera, but it is possible
to design an unreliable system. The big mistake is to depend on one camera
body of any kind.

The only special equipment that I may use for high-altitude work is
an ultraviolet (UV) filter. You may find yourself stopping down an extra stop
if you are over 2135 m (7000 ft) high because the light is brighter. However,
aside from these two corrections the work is fairly ordinary. The closest
thing to true special-effects work that I have done at high altitudes is with a
ski-mounted camera. This idea came to me in one of those great flashes that
takes about a year to get over. Some of the pictures have been quite fantastic,
and in spite of the fact that I have made very little money from them, I think
it was worth it. If you are going to mount a camera on a ski, a bicycle, an
automobile bumper, or whatever, you must do it securely. The idea of
mounting a camera in an odd place is valid because it gives another view of
our surroundings. "Another view" is properly one of the great objectives of
photography. It is fun to see feet walking down the boulevard from a
position just behind them, shot with an ultra-wide-angle lens. Shoes and
legs can be very expressive, and we rarely see them from some of the angles
the camera can achieve. It could also be very valid to mount a camera on a
pole and take a high wide-angle view of people as they meet and move
relative to one another, changing their postures as they talk. A sound track
could be made of what they are saying. These are special effects that can be
acheived by camera placement alone.

Shutter speeds

It may not be readily apparent that a high-speed shutter is a special effect,
but if you are aware of the way we actually see and that the eye does have an
effective shutter speed of about 1/30 sec. in normal light, then you will be
able to appreciate the fact that a small amount of motion blur is part of
normal vision. I would recommend that 1/30 sec. be used as a normal shutter
speed for a *totally normal* base image, but at this speed many photographers
inject camera motion and modify the image. In addition, few lenses now
stop down further than $f/22$, and with a typical film speed of ASA 64, it is
not possible to use a shutter speed of 1/30 sec. out of doors. A shutter speed
of 1/60 sec. is close enough, and in very bright sunlight the eye cycle is
probably more like 1/50 sec. anyway.

When you use higher shutter speeds, you are halting or freezing the
flow of events in a way that adds urgency to the image. Simultaneously

Low wide-angle camera positions can be very dramatic in action sequences and as establishing shots.

show two pictures of runners taken at 1/60 and 1/1000 sec. to individuals and see their reactions. I have not done a proper study of the effect, tabulating the response, but I have observed that images recorded at high shutter speeds have a very definite anxiety-producing effect on many people. The effect is usually slight unless the subject matter is very provocative, but it is there.

Conversely, very slow shutter speeds cause relaxation reactions, and this is especially true of scenes taken of flowing streams, waterfalls, and even twilight or nighttime traffic patterns of busy streets and freeways. The normal approach to making time exposures is to do the work under very low natural illumination, but there is an opportunity to use heavy neutral density filtration or low-speed emulsions and correction filters to make time exposures in normal daylight. The few images of these kinds that I have seen and produced were done for very special purposes. In the city you can, with some cooperation on the part of the subject, have an older person sitting on a park bench or bus bench while the rest of the world continues about in its frantic pace. In a two-exposure sequence, for example, the people in a train station may stand still as the train arrives, blurring into view, and then when the train comes to rest, the people are a blur. In the forest, a rabbit will freeze for many seconds while your open shutter records the movements of the flowers, grasses, and even the trees. The slow shutter can be a world in reverse, showing something of reality that we only see through the eye of the camera.

Slide sandwiches

Slide sandwiches give us yet another way of seeing, one in which objects can be juxtaposed in abnormal ways. This is an important technique because of a primary method of analysis—comparison. We compare the length of an object with the length of an arbitrary standard we call a ruler. We compare the weight or mass of objects with other arbitrary standards. Because it is the nature of this reality that we cannot literally see two things together, the technique of sandwiching is important.

I originally began sandwiching slides when I was trying to come up with an interesting visual from a large number of scenic ski pictures. Later, I found it to be a good transition technique in filmstrip work because we usually had thin outtakes and the need of a transition frame to bridge sequences. As a general rule, if you are going to shoot slides intended for a sandwich, you must have a background that does not contain much detail and a subject slide that has one sharp object in the center or a light area. Or, one picture must form a natural mat for the subject matter in the second frame. By far, the most effective sandwich of this kind that I have ever seen was made by the Los Angeles photographer Joey Fisher. The matting frame was a close-up of a white daisy in a dark background and a child's face was superimposed behind it. The composition is such that the child's nose is replaced by the center button of the daisy. The total effect is somewhat comical, but it is a very appropriate rendition of the curiosity of childhood as seen by an adult.

Really effective sandwiches take some planning unless you are working on a large project, like a series of educational filmstrips, in which you are going to have many thin outtakes. Unfortunately, for the sandwiching process, your efficiency always rises during one of these large productions. At the beginning you will have many bracketed frames, but you will begin to find which exposures work and just shoot those. I have known photographers who adhered to a 5:1 shooting ratio, bracketing by half stops all through a project. This is an utter waste of time, materials, and energy. In a large filmstrip project, or when shooting a lot of photography of the same kind, it is possible to get very close to 1:1. Having great heaps of outtakes in most cases means one thing: *something is wrong.*

Most slide mounts are quite easy to pull apart, but some caution is needed because the film may rip if great force is used.

Tape the first image in the mount. Install the second image over the first after it has been thoroughly cleaned. Tape the second frame of film in place before sealing.

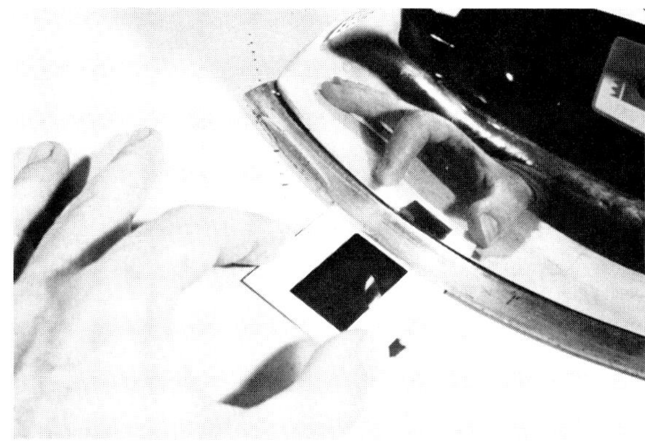

Then iron the slide on all four sides to seal the two pieces of film in place.

A sandwich must involve two layers of film, and at its very best it will never be totally sharp in projection or enlargement. Theoretically, it would be far better to make the combined images in camera on one piece of film as a multiple exposure. I have made some very effective images this way, but the planning and precision needed are more than the average producer wants to contend with, and there are hazards in the process. Some of the current 35 mm cameras will allow multiple exposures without moving the film, but most still require rewinding the previously exposed frame or overriding the double-exposure prevention mechanism by pushing the rewind release while cocking the shutter. Neither of these techniques is satisfactory because neither is reliable. And, neither is really compatible with the production of the planned multiple exposure because the objects of the two separate images are usually in two different places at two different times.

Multiple exposures

The solution to all of these problems is found in a marking pen and a piece of paper. The pen is used to register the film in the camera, and the paper is used for careful notes of what is on each frame of the film. The classic multiple-exposure exercise, and the only one I've seen work well virtually every time, is that of placing the moon in odd places on the film. Audiences and contest judges are very receptive to this kind of image. Every time I've used one of these pictures in a show, it got half the "Oh's" and "Ah's" heard during the entire show. If you watch the major contests, you will see one of these slides in every group of winners.

The very first thing to do when setting up your camera for this work is to inspect the film-advance gear usually found on the right side of the film path near the take-up spool. Push the film rewind release and rotate the gear to see if you can find some screw, indentation, mark, or other feature that will permit you to reset this gear in exactly the same position every time you load a roll of film. If there is no such mark on the gear, you may want to make a small one with a nail file, awl, or scribe. The objective is to be able to set as much of the mechanism as possible at a "zero" or starting position so that the film can be advanced as precisely as possible. Next, load a roll of film in the normal manner, but make a registration mark on the back of the roll at the right-side end of the film-guide rails or some other convenient, repeatable place. This should be done when the camera is cocked, thus starting its counter at zero, and all internal gearing is engaged. At this point close the camera, advance it to the starting frame, and begin exposing moon images. The moon is perfect for this kind of work because it is very bright in an otherwise dark sky, and a proper exposure for it will be 1/60 sec. at *f*/16 or *f*/11. However, you may want to make the moon brighter to give it a bit of a halo.

On the paper, note where you have placed each of the moon exposures. I recommend putting them in the upper left- or right-hand corner, depending on the available background material. You may want to note which lens or lenses were used to record the moon shots, but I recommend the longest focal-length lens for all the moon images. If you have a 500 mm lens, it is about the ideal length and also the limit. A 200 mm lens will also work well, and the 135 mm is short but will do in a pinch.

The background subject matter can be anything from a sunset, which produces the highly unlikely image of a lit moon against its source, through successively deeper twilights, to nighttime exposures of city lights best taken from a hill or tall building. When you reinstall the film, just remember to return the advance gear to its original position, load the film with the

Registering each roll of film, in this case to the end of the guide rail above and the white tape mark below, will allow you to rewind and re-install rolls of film for multiple exposures, flashing, multiple images, and other special effects.

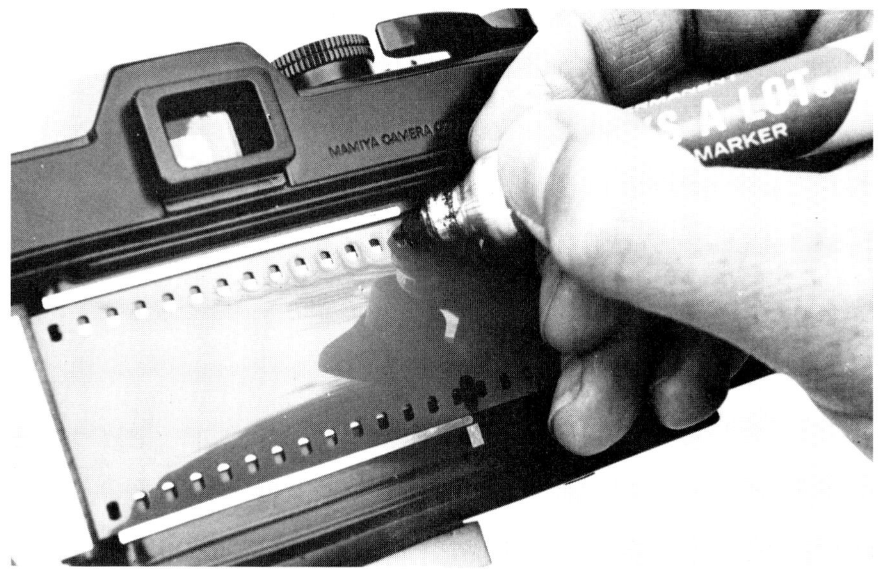

mechanism cocked, and realign the marking-pen line with the rail end or other feature that you originally used to create a starting position.

I align all rolls of film in this manner as a matter of course. It is not very necessary when you are shooting in your own home area and have several camera bodies on hand, but if you are on the road or on location, the registration of each roll of film is a good safety procedure, and it expands the capabilities of your system. In the early 1960s it became apparent to me that one of the great failings of the 35 mm camera system was that it did not have an interchangeable film capability. With the systems available at that time, you could change lenses and finder systems, and add extension rings, Barlow-lens focal extenders, light sources, and so on. However, when you put a roll of film into the camera, that was it until you took it out. This may have been all right for the photographer who wanted to use only one kind of film, but in that period I was using seven different emulsions, four color and three black-and-white. Thus, out of pure need I hatched what I call "The Interchangeable Film System," and it was the subject of the first article I wrote for the photographic press, appearing in *U.S. Camera* in the February 1967 issue.

In essence, the system is that of simply registering each roll of film in the manner described, permitting you to take it out of the camera at any point. The system coincidentally permits double exposures and flashing, a technique that is used to increase film speed, but the main benefit is that of freeing the camera body at any point, so it can be used to expose another emulsion better suited to the light and conditions.

Flashing

Flashing is a technique that appears in magazines with regularity, and it is always greeted as some new, incredible advance, now normally involved with a complicated mechanical system. Flashing is a simple procedure if you register film because you can run the film back through the camera and do it to only certain frames, thereby not committing the entire roll to a procedure that may ruin it. What makes flashing work is that a photographic exposure is a range of values spread along a curve of values correlating the exposure given with the quanta captured. An additional bit of light given uniformly to the film will simply move all the values up the scale, rendering those in the lower sections more usable. The procedure is really a bit silly when applied to negative materials because it does not change the relative value of the exposures, contrary to what some have written about it. The technique does not "slide everything up the characteristic curve"; it moves the entire curve vertically. Thus, the toe of the curve is still a toe, but it is taller. However, the technique of flashing does work with reversal materials, and it is especially important to photographers who are going to project first-generation work. In addition, it can be done very simply.

Again, reregister the film you have previously shot, and with the lens cap in place, crank through the previously exposed frames that you do not want to flash. When you arrive at the frame or frames to be flashed, remove the lens cap and install a filter holder with a UV filter in place. Add one or two circles cut from the whitest 25 percent cotton bond typing paper you can find, and place them in the filter holder. If you're going to do a lot of this kind of work, you may want to have a filter-size circle cut from white Plexiglas because this is more permanent. In either case the basic technique is the same. You aim the UV filter and typing paper or Plexiglas sandwich at the sun and determine what the meter would call a normal exposure, i.e., the combination of shutter speed and aperture that will center the indicator needle or light-emitting diode for the exposure index of the film in the camera. I hasten to add that this combination is created for the *original exposure index of the film* and not the one you desire in the end. Once that setting is found, you must reduce the actual flashing exposure by six or seven stops and keep the lens on the infinity setting during all readings and flashing exposures.

If you are working with a high-speed film, you may find that four or five thicknesses of typing paper are needed to reduce the input of the light. Sunlight should always be your light source, as other kinds of light do not have the correct color balance to do the flashing perfectly. Other kinds of light may *appear* to be daylight, but their color balance is not the same as that of daylight. These other light sources will work, but they are not ideal. You can, however, inject a non-linear color correction that will allow you to use a light source other than daylight to obtain perfect flashing.

You can also use a gray card to determine a normal exposure if you are working with very high-speed film, but it has been my experience that Kodak gray cards are never color pure and usually have a magenta error.

However you go about it, the flashing exposure is meant to be from one-half to one-and-one-half percent, and never more than two percent, of the original exposure in terms of middle gray. This is the reason the camera meter is used to determine the exposure level; it reads everything in terms of middle gray. The increase in film speed is about double, but some photographers report a four-time increase in the upper ranges of flashing, six stops down the scale instead of seven, with the highest speed materials. With the system the speed of Kodak high-speed Ektachrome film, daylight type, which is normally rated at ASA 200, goes to 400 and to 800 with normal processing. However, the important point is that this is a selective process, and you can actually have two film speeds in one roll of film! This is a capability that few photographers need, but it is a nice trick to have in the bag, and one you have for the price of a marking pen, a piece of paper, and a few other things you probably already have.

Slide duplicating and posterization

When all things are considered, the best way to handle multiple-image problems is with a multiple-image duplicating setup. Slide duplicating has always been a difficult thing, because a picture of a picture is not the same thing as the picture of the original object or objects. In addition, slide duplication as a field was long ago led down the path to difficulty by a bad idea, a penny-wise attitude, and much armchair engineering. The bad idea was that a diffuse light source, because it would optically erase scratches and dust, is best. The penny-wise attitude has always meant the cheapest possible unit would be constructed, again resulting in a diffuser light source.

Some years ago I went to work on the problem of slide duplication, reasoning that the difficulty lay in the diffuse light source because this edge-softening light would pass through the highlights in greater quantities and wash out what detail had been recorded. I noted that most duplicates were actually more dense in the highlight region than the originals because the cameramen would try to retain the detail by reducing the exposure. Since the edge-softening effect is a function of exposure, this was the only correction they could apply, but it also reduced the range of the exposure, rendering the lower-end, darker regions muddy. In compensation some labs would flash the film, but this simply moved the response curve vertically, negating the reduction correction.

In my first attempt to correct the situation, I polarized the light, and this increased the performance of the system by 20 percent in terms of lines per millimetre transfer. The next stage of development included adding a condenser and removing the diffuser. I did try point-source experiments, but quickly found that this is going too far. To explain the effect I have developed a theory of source-light contrast which is yet incomplete, but the result has been a duplicating light source that is far better than anything on the market. At the present time it is a breadboard setup using an enlarger lamp, a condenser, a filter pack with one or two polarizers, the subtractive filters needed, and a Kodak IR (infrared) cutoff filter No. 108. The contrast of the light varies by changing the position of the enlarger lamp relative to the focal point of the condenser. When the center of the bulb is at the focal point,

126

the beam is collimated, thus producing the highest possible contrast of the system. Adding polarizers increases the apparent contrast of the system, I believe, by ordering the light. What is needed, and this is the subject of the current development program, is a contrast metering system so that the most appropriate light can be used for the various subjects and emulsions.

The film is handled in this system in much the same manner as in any camera. It is registered and then run through the apparatus with notes taken on each frame or set of frames. Then, the film is rewound, registered, and the second images are added. We usually prepare a set of frames of varying densities so we can pick the best or use several in a sequence. The system gives complete control, and now that we have managed to increase the quality of the product so substantially, the results are acceptable. Still, a duplicate will never match an original even if the exposure is correct and the lab has done its work properly.

One product of the slide duplicator that is not terribly dependent on quality and can only be made this way is the effect called *posterization.* The method that I will outline was first developed by the Los Angeles photographer Jim Zuckerman. The images that work best with the system have considerable detail and a wide range of densities. You have probably seen examples of this type of effect in photographic magazines, and the effect is usually done with color prints, working from a negative or internegative, many emulsions, chemical systems, and a great deal of time.

Jim Zuckerman saw a shortcut through all this using a slide duplicator. His process was that of making a copy of the original on Kodak Ektachrome infrared film shot at an estimated exposure index of 50. Then he copied the original onto one of the Kodak Ektachrome films, but he processed it as a negative in Kodak's C 22 process. Where the infrared film essentially reported an image of reds, oranges, and yellows, the other Ektachrome negative, without the usual negative orange mask, reported it in blues and greens. Then, Jim made yet another copy on Kodalith film. The Ektachrome negative exposures and Kodalith exposures have to be determined experimentally because there are now too many variables to quote figures. As a mid-range starting point I can tell you that the Ektachrome negative will have an effective film speed of about four times its normal exposure index, and the Kodalith will have a film speed of about one.

The results are sandwiched in any combination that seems to work, as there are no stringent rules in the posterization process. The images can be very strong attention-getters when used alone, but their real power comes when they are used in sequences. The ideal projection or display occurs with

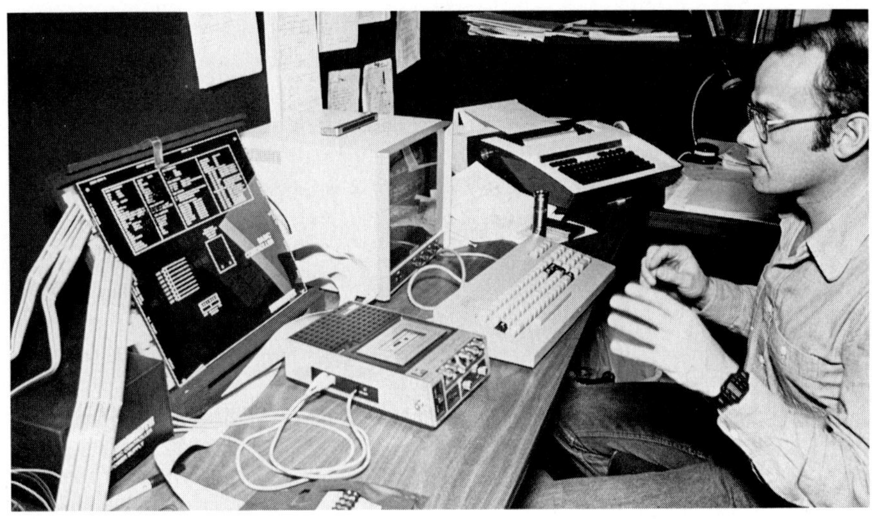

Cameraman Jim Villeaux and the Filmation camera animating system. The system was developed from existing computer hardware for the purpose of generating film special effects.

any kind of dissolve system, slide projector, two video tape recorders mixing to a master tape, or an animation camera "lap" dissolve sequence. This is one special-effect system that the motion-picture people have really overlooked in the main. It is best done with a sequence of still images rephotographed in several emulsions which are used and processed in strange ways. This process cannot be done with motion-picture camera systems alone. A still or animation camera system will have to be involved in the process.

MAGIC

Suspensions

The art of producing effects beyond the normal human powers is defined as magic. In the audiovisual business this usually involves making things fly for the benefit of the camera. As is always the rule, the simplest way to accomplish an objective is best. Thus, many of these effects are done by the very simple process of suspending objects by lines that are rendered invisible by any of several methods. Because film prints in motion-pictures or filmstrips barely have 10 percent of the resolution of the original material,

128

you can get away with the most incredible suspension systems imaginable. Most of these systems make use of nylon line of the kind used in fly fishing rigs, and it is the thinnest kind available, usually two-pound test. This figure indicates the breaking strength of the line and also tells us that the objects to be suspended had better be light in weight. In some cases the objects will be nothing more than posterboard models or mounted photographs of the actual object that is to fly in space.

In all suspension systems it is absolutely necessary to have at least two, and preferably three, lines on the object to be "flown." Objects on one line never stop moving, and they move in a way that virtually points to the suspension spot as they swing back and forth in pendulum fashion. A second line from approximately a 90 degree angle usually cures this tendency, but with this system there is still one plane in which the object can swing. A third line at approximately 90 degrees to both of the other lines will settle the object in space and give you a lot of control over it as well. As a general rule, the time you spend properly mounting objects to be suspended can be multiplied by four in terms of what it will save you when the photography starts. There are few things more nerve-wracking than having to wait for a complicated suspension system to come to rest in a boiling hot studio in which you've had to turn off the air conditioning and seal doors and windows to kill the breezes. A few extra lines mean that the photography can be done quickly and well in a studio where the air conditioning runs, the radio plays, and life continues normally.

Nylon fishing line works well when you are doing an exterior shot of a flying box, toy, aircraft model, or ball because it has a color that goes well with that of the sky. Normally, the fishing line is pale blue or sufficiently transparent to be essentially invisible to the camera. But, the round form of the line itself forms a rod-shaped lens that can gather light and produce a bright line along its length. For this reason the light over the suspension will often have to be controlled with a giant screen, usually called a *scrim.* The least expensive of these can be made with a king-size bedsheet tied at each corner and mounted on four poles.

Light control is the main reason that so many suspensions are done in photographic studios. But unless you have an enormous barn of a studio, the scale of the work will have to be reduced, and if you get too close to the lines, they will be visible. The finest material available for doing close-up suspensions is dental floss. This product is made of the finest, longest nylon fibers produced. The product must be teased apart with great care, but a bit of practice with dry fingers and a couple of needles will soon yield a few metres of fiber that you cannot see at a distance of 0.9 m (3 ft). In addition,

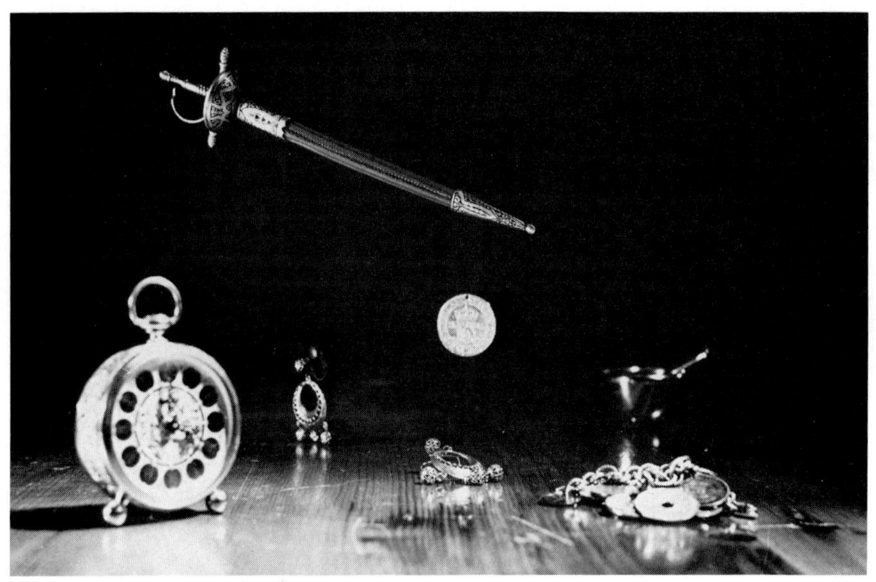

Special-effects suspension accomplished with single fibers teased from dental floss. This material is virtually invisible to the close-up camera and will allow small objects to be manipulated.

the fiber is strong.

In less demanding circumstances black thread can be used in front of black "outer space" backgrounds because this product is far easier to handle. All nylon monofilament lines, and especially the very, very fine ones, have a tendency to twist and kink. When the fibers are teased out of the main thread, they must be installed in the suspension immediately or taped at each end to a long board or cabinet. Ordinary thread, having many fibers in a bundle, does not tend to twist in this manner and can be handled with considerable abandon. A small spool of this material stuck in a shirt pocket enables you to perform all kinds of suspension magic in the studio.

If you are working with a background color other than black, the suspension lines will have to be the same color as the background and lit to the same intensity as the background. It is very difficult to match paint color to thread color, and the only way I've ever done it is to paint a small board or panel the same color as the background and go to the notions counter at a large department store or sewing shop and pick through the samples until something matches.

The classic mounting system in motion-picture work has become the rod because it is much stiffer than thread, and if it is mounted correctly behind the object, it is utterly invisible. Rods should always be painted the same color as the background, and for safety reasons, the metal tubes are much preferred over wooden dowels because they are much more rigid.

It is clear now that more and more special-effects motion-picture work is going to be done with computer-controlled camera and mounting systems, where the effects are built in a series of passes. Having the object on a stiff rod simplifies the computer programming for the shot. Rod systems should be used in any case when the object being photographed has to spin or turn and is being seen in a dissolve or animated sequence. Usually, having the rod the same color as the background and lighting it carefully will not be enough camouflage to render it invisible. This means that a *matt,* or series of matts, will have to be generated to perfect the image. Matts are the ultimate weapon in this phase of the special-effects business, and the making and using of them will be outlined very shortly.

The last suspension method in regular use is that of the *glass stage.* For slide work this is usually a 61 × 91.4 cm (2′ × 3′) piece of "water clear" glass with ground edges to prevent cuts. You won't believe the price of this material compared to that of regular glass, but there is no substitute for it. Plate glass is very thick, heavy, and hard to handle, but the feature that ruins it for color photography is its green color. Objects photographed through the glass will have a different color, by about 20 points of green, compared to those mounted on the front side of the plate. This means that there is no way to correct for the color balance throughout the shot when plate glass has been used.

Lighting for glass-stage work is very tricky because the direction of the key light has to be almost exactly perpendicular to the plane of the glass. This can only be accomplished by making an indicator from a dowel or soda straw glued to a cardboard square about 30 cm (1 ft) on each side. The straw or dowel must be perpendicular to the cardboard. When the indicator is attached to the glass with masking tape, the correct position for the key light can be found by adjusting the indicator until the shadow of the straw disappears. This occurs when the key light is exactly perpendicular to the glass.

The fill lights can be placed approximately, but their distance from the stage has to be determined by an incident-light exposure meter. Take the key-light reading and then shut the key light off before setting the fill lights. Set one fill light at a time and adjust each one so the output is more than two stops down from the level of the key light. If the fill-light outputs exceed this level, the object will produce reflections that will be recorded on film. You will find that working with a glass stage is difficult, frustrating, and nerve-wracking, but there are times when a glass stage can be the very best way to get a shot.

In one of the most ambitious shots I have ever scheduled, we used a glass stage to hold the parts of an "exploded" transistor radio, which would appear to come together in front of a setting sun as the brilliant orb settled on the tip of a radio-station antenna high above Beverly Hills, California. I had found the perfect location for this shot by first noting the magnetic compass bearing for sunset and then scouting the most likely area with compass in hand.

The sun is about one-half degree wide and only moves north or south one-quarter degree per day, depending on the season. Thus, an observed heading for the sunset worked very well for several days because few hand-bearing compasses are accurate for measurements less than one degree.

On the appointed day we were at the location one hour before the first shot of the sequence and had the basic setup made in about 30 minutes. The fill light was to be provided by reflectors, the output of which would be controlled by position and dulling spray. Unfortunately, reflectors produce an intense beam if they are not handled carefully, and the angle of their output changed with the changing angle of the sun. Problems notwithstanding, we kept the apparatus working throughout the sequence and got the shots. I rushed the film off to the best and most reliable lab in town. The next day I received the slides, but the roll of film had been developed in the wrong chemical system. You could recognize the shots, but they were not usable.

Back on the mountain, but this time with two loaded cameras, we shot the sequence the next evening, and this time we took one roll to another lab while the second, back-up roll rested in the freezer. This time the lab did it right, and we didn't even bother to have the second roll processed. Very complicated special-effects work, the kind we call "magic," does need some kind of protection program, and I've found that the second camera body is about the only way to really guarantee the shot.

We've worked with just about every still film lab in Hollywood and several in large cities while doing location work. If you stay with a lab long enough, you can be absolutely sure something will get ruined or lost. Most color lab work is very simple, and you would think that anyone could do it with his or her eyes closed, but therein lies the problem. The work is boring, and often people don't pay full attention to what is going on in the tanks and on the machines. In addition, most labs will have a few people who really do know what is going on and who can make corrections if the process begins to fail, but most of the people working in the labs are not that familiar with the process.

Matts

When I began to develop more and more special-effects techniques, and the amount of time going into each exposure, to say nothing of an entire roll of film, was mounting rapidly, the thought of losing a roll produced sleepless nights or nightmares. What could be done to either simplify the processes or build some degree of protection directly into them? I also had long felt that there must be some better way to go about all of this to give more creative choices and a better utilization of the images. The ultimate weapon in all special-effects work is the *matt*. A matt is a dense black image in the shape of the object of interest. It is a silhouette, and it may be made any one of several ways; all are troublesome and some are expensive, but the results are fantastic.

Matts are generally made by contact printing film onto a sheet of Kodalith film, a super high-contrast black-and-white negative stock that has an utterly clear base. The gamma of this stock is *four*, which means that it is either off or on and in most cases will report any exposure as dead black. Exposure is so critical with this material that a correct exposure of say, 8 seconds may not be varied more than 1 or 2 seconds in either direction without producing a totally black or clear result when the sheet is processed. The film is orthochromatic, which means that it is not sensitive to red light, and while this means that it is handy to work with in the darkroom, it cannot be used to make matts for red subject matter. This is a very real handicap when doing outer-space special effects because so many rocket exhausts, lights, and other effects can be very effective in red. Kodalith film's blindness to red is the real reason that so many of these effects are done in white and blue-white.

Contact printing can be done in any darkroom equipped with an enlarger. The baseboard on which the film is to be placed should be covered with black paper, and the wood surface should be painted flat black. The film on which the printing is to be done, usually Kodalith film, is then placed emulsion-side up, and the film that is to be printed onto it is placed directly on the first film emulsion-side down. If the film to be printed is a slide, it must be removed from the mount and should be cleaned with an antistatic cloth. The same cloth may be gently wiped over the printing emulsion surface, and during the time of assembly liberal use of a rubber syringe, blower, or air hose will ensure that dust does not settle on one of the many surfaces involved.

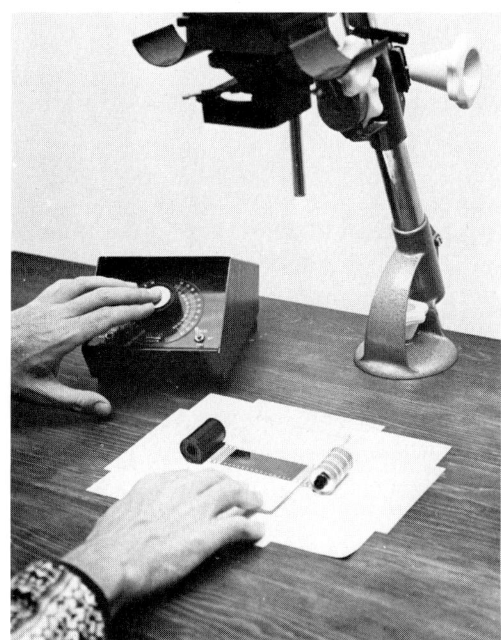

Contact printing onto film can be accomplished simply with two spools, an enlarger, and filter pack or color head. This method can be used to make slide productions.

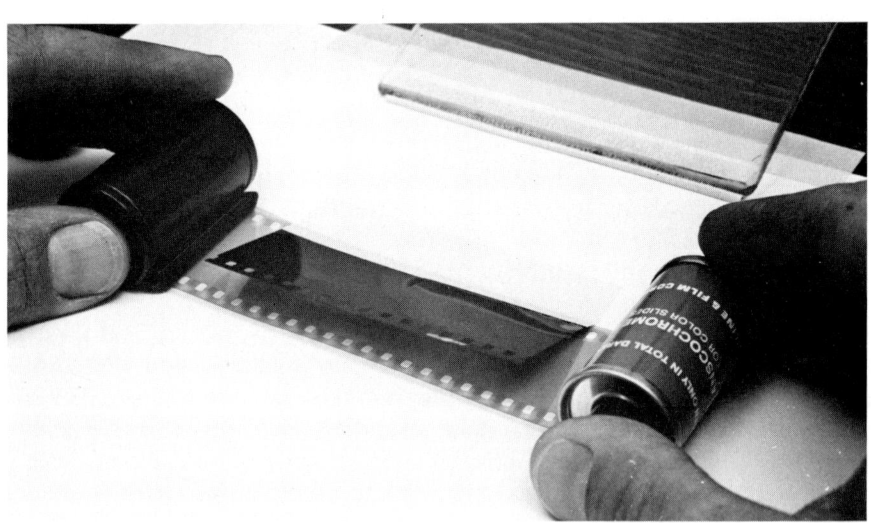

Place duplicating stock, masking film or Kodalith film, under a pair of un-mounted slides taped to the baseboard. In actual use, the enlarger baseboard is covered with black paper for antireflection purposes.

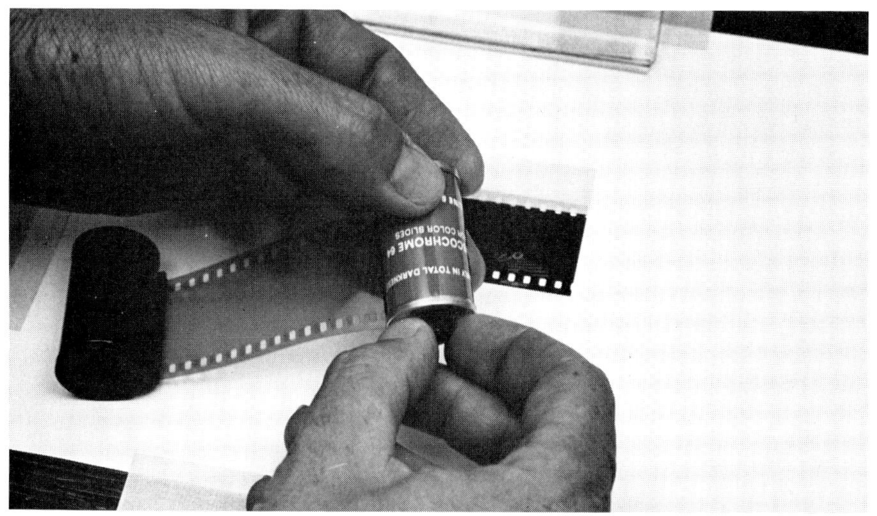

After exposure, wind the film into an empty take-up spool.

A glass platen should be rigged to cover the film during the actual exposure. With some luck and great care during the actual assembly, it is possible to print eight matts on a single sheet of 4" × 5" film. However, the great amount of work involved in the entire process, including the cutting, mounting in register, and so forth, caused an alternative to be developed that is done in camera.

Kodalith film can be exposed in a slide duplicator, but the exposure will take 10 to 30 seconds and can be arrived at initially only by experimentation, and later by experience. There is no way you can accurately meter the proper exposure to make a matt with this material because its exposure index is extremely low (about *one*), and its response is not panchromatic—it does not correlate to that of the cadmium sulfide meter circuit. In this case the only usable exposure meter is a piece of the film itself.

The other outstanding problem in making matts in camera is that most slide duplicators are set up to enlarge the image three percent as a safety factor to avoid duplicating the slide mount. This arrangement will not do in making matts; the reproduction ratio simply *has* to be exactly 1:1. Accomplishing this can be difficult, but we have developed a technique that allows us to tune the slide duplicator specifically for this work. It uses two pieces of film for making the adjustment and can usually be accomplished in a few minutes. In essence, you make two copies of a field chart on a high-contrast color reversal stock like Kodachrome film. One copy is left in the mount, and the other is removed from the mount and stored in a way that will keep it absolutely flat. (We keep ours in a large dictionary facing the page on which the word *Kodachrome* is defined.)

The mounted slide of the field chart is put in the slide duplicator in the ordinary manner, and the back of the camera is opened. The shutter is locked open on "B" (bulb), and the second, unmounted piece of film is put in the focal plane and held in place with two small pieces of masking tape carefully applied to the film and the upper- and lower-limit rails. The focal-plane-mounted film is mounted so the center lines agree both vertically and horizontally. This may mean that you will have to lift the slide slightly or remove some of the bottom of the mount to let it fall far enough into the holder. However this is accomplished, the two pairs of center crosshairs must be superimposed. Now you can move the lens and body back and forth until the central-area grid squares or rectangles agree. You will not be able to make the outer-edge rectangles match perfectly due to barrel distortion of the copy lens. Don't despair. All of them have it. However, the amount of barrel distortion can be reduced by using a proper copy lens or an enlarger lens. These optics are designed to work in close ranges where barrel distortion is especially apparent, and their formulas have been idealized for this work.

When the apparatus has been aligned and the normal magnification factor eliminated, you are ready to shoot matts. The very nice thing about shooting matts on 35 mm stock is that the registration problem often drops out of the equation. If the camera body is designed to place the images in a standard fashion, with the space between any two images falling precisely between two perforations, the matt and the original will be registered. This means that the original and the matt can be placed in two peg-registered mounts and used without any further adjustment. The only difficulty with this is that some of the pegged mounts are very thick, and you cannot get two of them into most of the slide-duplicator holders. This is the reason that we normally mount all special-effects originals and matts in cardboard by hand. This may sound tricky, but in practice it can be quite simple.

Matts, masks, many elements in posterizations, and black-lettered titles are hand-mounted in cardboard mounts because they are cheap, and the process works. When mounting matts the secret of success is to first place the original image in its mount with tape so that the film is firmly in place. Sometimes the iron does not seal the mount sufficiently to lock the film in place, and if it can move a little, the matt won't work. Next, the second mount that will carry the matt is placed over the first while the second mount is still open and flat. The bottom of this mount and the left side of the first mount are firmly pushed against a tabletop to be sure that they are aligned, and the two mounts are held together with a strong spring clip. The matt is then placed over the image and tacked in place with small pieces of cellophane tape cut for that purpose. Generally, two pieces of tape will locate the matt sufficiently for the sealing operation.

Once sealed with an iron, the matt is ready to be checked. This should be done in the slide duplicator in which the matt will be used. When the original image and the matt are in the slide holder, *no light* should come through the sandwich if the matt is going to work perfectly. You may see a halo around an edge, but adjusting the matt and the original in the duplicator may cure it if you have inadvertently let them slip apart in the installation procedure.

When the special-effects image is to be made, the matt is installed in the slide duplicator *in front* of the background slide into which the image is to be placed. The matt image is dead black, and when the first copy exposure is made, the background image will be recorded in all areas but those blacked out by the matt. In the next exposure, which must be done without moving the film, the original image from which the matt was made will have to be dropped precisely into the unexposed area. In most of this work these original objects are shot in front of dead-black backgrounds, so they are self-matted. But in some cases, special matts must be prepared to block out the background of the original. There are several processes for making these matts, and none of them is simple.

The rotoscope technique is a method of preparing matts, titles, and special-effects images. The technique can be made to work very well, but it is time consuming. In essence, the rotoscope technique is simply that of projecting a slide onto a drawing surface for the purpose of making a very precise copy, outline, or placement of title letters, figures, or arrows that are going to be part of the final image. But in using this procedure to make a matt, the outline of the figure to be isolated is copied, and either the figure or the area around it is blacked out totally, depending on whether Kodalith or Kodachrome film is going to be used to make the trapping matt.

Drawing an accurate trapping matt with a rotoscope is as simple or difficult as the subject matter, and copying it in the right scale, not too large or small, is usually a matter of trial and error in correctly adjusting the camera. We have also made trapping matts directly on the film of an original, but we usually do it on a duplicate with the Mars Staedtler pen and Rapidograph Waterproof Black Drawing Ink. The 0.35 mm tip seems to work very well in most of our applications, but much narrower tips are available in art supply stores in which the pens are sold. It is best to make a series of duplicates if you are new to this procedure. Remove the film from the slide mount and tape it to a 4" × 5" glass sheet so the film can be rotated on a flat light box. Do the blacking on the backing because the gelatin side will swell when it is wet and be rather easily damaged. You will be amazed at how accurately you can work in these small areas.

We also use the Mars Staedtler pen and Rapidograph ink to patch up 35 mm matts that are not quite right. The Kodalith film's response is so critical that it will sometimes miss an area that you want blacked. Therefore, make a sandwich of the original and the processed Kodalith matt, backing-side up, and carefully black out the areas you want to block.

These systems are really a lot of trouble, and ones that we do not use unless we have to. In a typical filmstrip series we may have to resort to this kind of work perhaps once or a few times. In a series dealing with African animals, we needed to place a meat-eating lion in a grassy area and could only succeed in getting a picture of one eating hamburger on a road in an animal park. A picture of an open grassy area very like those in Africa plus the trap-matted lion produced the needed image. In another problem situation we needed a shot of a great white shark underwater. Because none of these animals are in captivity (they're rarely seen, thoroughly unpredicta-ble, and potentially dangerous), we shot a model in a museum. The background included several other nearby exhibits, which we blacked out with the pen. We made the Kodalith matt optically and dropped the shark into a kelp bed. In this project involving nearly 400 images, this was the only image for which we went to the trouble of the full process.

Front projection

Special-effects work can include front projection, and while a full treatment of this subject is a bit beyond the scope of this book (only because of the variations in the equipment), the theory of the process is quite simple, and some recommendations can be made for improving the result if you are involved in it. In this process a beam splitter is placed in front of the camera lens, and at right angles to the camera lens axis, a slide projector casts an image to the beam splitter which then reflects it along the axis of the camera lens. At a convenient point in this setup, a lenticular screen, or other highly reflective screen made for this purpose, is placed, and the slide that is being projected is seen in the camera lens with incredible realism. If an object or person is then placed in front of the screen and lit properly, the object or person will appear to become part of the image. However, a photograph of this mixture of picture and person will show that the picture is really from two sources because there is strong dupe quality to the background and a normal contrast and texture range for the person.

The cure for this rendition is to pick the background subject matter very carefully and to be sure that it is either of low contrast naturally or has been manipulated to have low contrast. This does not have to be a problem because most backgrounds for people should have low contrast anyway. A forest background can be difficult unless the forest was shot on an overcast day. The light in a forest is of very high contrast, ranging from brilliant white, to middle tones, to black. Backgrounds that include printing or signs that should be readable can be troublesome because the plane of the background is usually several metres in back of the subject, and in a studio setup you may be shooting with a fairly open lens to use a shutter speed of 1/60 sec. The great cure for depth of field is any one of the several front-projection outfits that use electronic flash for projecting the image as well as lighting the subject. These tend to perform very well in all respects, giving a good rendition to the background subject matter and plenty of depth of field, but the photographer does need to be familiar with them. The only effective exposure meter for this type of apparatus is a piece of film, and these front-projection outfits require several rounds of testing before they are used for the first time.

Special-effects work is often complicated, but the results are exciting, satisfying, and lucrative. If you are going to do much special-effects work, it is necessary to allow two or three times as much time for it, and be prepared for some big disappointments. When some of these systems work well, the result for you is a great feeling of power and union with the medium. Then, it's worth it.

12

Sound

Night fades into dawn and we see on a hill a curving road set with homes, yards, fences, and garages. Instantly, the chirping birds stop as yowling cats and clattering garbage cans pierce the morning. A car starts, appears at the bottom of the hill, and climbs through the scene with a sporty exhaust tone as it navigates the curves. The theme fades in, and we see title and production credits for the show. This simple opening, done from a single camera position, is dynamic because of sound. Sound has traditionally been the last frontier of the audiovisual media. It was tacked onto motion pictures in the 30s, added to filmstrips in the 50s, and is not yet regularly broadcast in stereo for television. Sound remains the most open creative dimension in all audiovisual media because it is not studied or understood to the depth of visual images. And yet, so very much is left to the sound track.

Most of the information in a sound track is transmitted by voice, whether the production is an educational film or a dramatic presentation. But, most emotion is expressed as music or musical sounds. All sound in an audiovisual sound track should be handled as if it were music. An understanding of the rules of music will permit you to make a sequence like that described above either pleasant or grating. The story that follows dictates which style you choose, melodic or dissonant. However, to make the choice the fundamental question "What is music?" must be answered.

THE HISTORY AND THEORY OF MUSIC

Music is the art of organizing sound to produce an aesthetic response. Inasmuch as there is no natural organization of sound in this universe, all music is synthetic. According to legend our musical system was developed in antiquity by a few Greek philosophers. Included in this group was the great mathematician Pythagoras (580-500 BC), who is known to have made studies of the vibrations of strings. In spite of the fact that there is no written record of his work, we can be sure that Pythagoras sought a musical system based on a natural interval, or division, of tone. There is only one such relationship that these men could have discovered with the equipment available in their times, and that is the modes of vibration: wholes, halves, thirds, quarters, fifths, and sixths.

If a string is touched at a mid, third, quarter, fifth, or sixth point, at the moment it is plucked it begins to vibrate in the appropriate illustrated mode. The locations at which the strings appear to cross, both in this illustration and on an instrument, are called *nodal points*. This technique is still used by modern stringed-instrument players to produce harmonics. The halves mode produces what is called the *first harmonic,* and it was understood in antiquity that this tone was of twice the frequency of the whole mode of vibration. The tones produced by the other modes are not simple multiples of the first, but instead are separate, distinct tones. It is important to know that each tone in the series is substantially weaker in volume than the one before. The earliest stringed instruments, types of harps, were tuned in thirds, which is to say that the musician simply sounded the *second harmonic,* the thirds mode of vibration, and tuned the adjacent lower string to it. Even today modern stringed instruments are

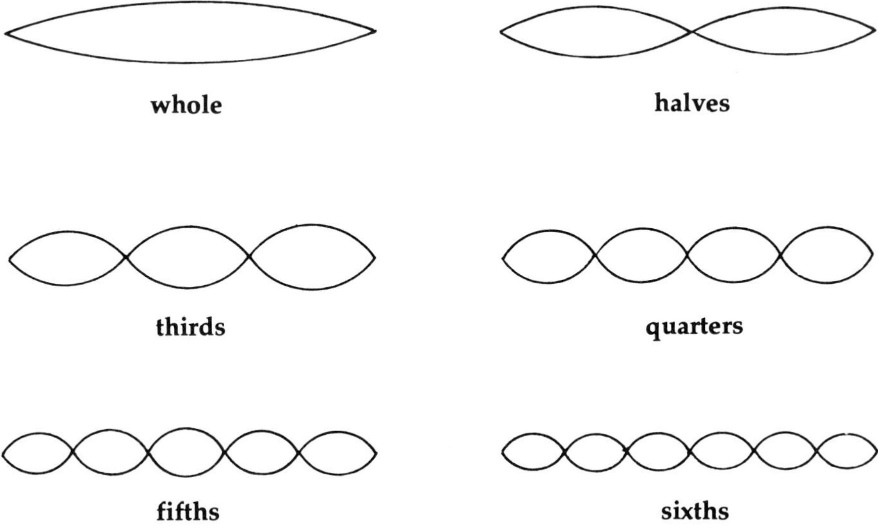

tuned in this fashion. The harp was then used to accompany a song, where it made an occasional reference tone for a vocalist who would modulate randomly through a composition uncomplicated by a musical scale. If Pythagoras and his contemporaries had any musical sensitivity at all, their motivation to improve the situation must have been intense. The streets of the ancient Greek cities were literally jammed with singing itinerant poets wailing away at all hours.

At this point, in the sixth century BC, the western musical scale consisted of two tones—the fundamental tone and a tone that was about 80 percent on the way, in terms of frequency, to what now is called *the octave.* A change in harp construction, the addition of a sounding box which amplified the tones, made it apparent that other harmonics, and tones, were available. In modern terms, the third harmonic, the quarters mode of vibration, is *one full tone* from the second harmonic, and the fourth harmonic is *one semitone* from the third harmonic. We can be sure that the Greek philosophers did not hear the fifth harmonic, string vibration in the sixths mode, or things would be very different in music today. In addition, it can be demonstrated that only the very best of the modern stringed instruments will produce an audible fifth harmonic. On a fine classical guitar the fifth harmonic can be found about halfway between the second and third frets if the instrument is capable of producing it. The discovery of the interval between the third and fourth harmonics was greeted rather like the discovery of the atom. Whereas the atom is the smallest distinct unit of matter, the interval was thought to be the unit tone in a natural musical scale. The development of instruments then moved in the direction of fingerboards, where the nodal points could be marked and ultimately where frets could be placed.

When frets were placed at the visible nodal points and the string was pressed to that point on the fingerboard, a pluck produced the same musical tone as the harmonic, but it was loud like the sound of a string vibrating in the whole mode. Harmonics are relatively weak in loudness and generally not usable in playing, but the placing of frets at the nodal points produced a musical scale of four tones: the fundamental, second, third, and fourth harmonics. However, the sounds of the tones indicated that the scale was uneven, and the regularity of the fret placement suggested that the keyboard could be further divided. An unknown instrument maker discovered that if he were to divide the string length by 18, subtract the dividend from the length, and place a fret, he could continue the process, landing also on the fret positions placed by harmonics, and divide the musical interval between the fundamental tone of the string and the first harmonic by 12 equal tones.

142

This was the first fully colored, or chromatic, scale, and it was a great technical advance in music. But it created another problem: There were too many tones!

Human perception is fairly limited in its ability to discriminate audio frequency, and as luck would have it, the philosophers built their system with an interval just below the ear's ability to make a clear distinction and to enable recollection. The most obvious simplification would have been to divide the chromatic scale in half, playing every other tone, but experiments in this direction indicated that such a simplified scale was a grim thing to hear. You can duplicate this scale by playing the tones A, B, C#, E♭, F, G, and A' from the present scale, and it is at this point that it must be said that music is something with which one must play. Furthermore, the instrument does not have to be expensive; a dime-store xylophone can teach you a lot about music.

Dividing the chromatic scale precisely in half would have produced a seven-tone system wherein the seventh tone would have been the first harmonic. But experiments with "modes," an early name for scales, indicated that there was a more fruitful path, or set of paths, through the chromatic confusion. The basic idea was to pick 8 of the 12 tones and define them as whole tones with those in between labeled half tones, or sharps and flats. Unfortunately, the system has a confusion factor built into it because the interval between two of the whole tones simply has to be a half tone. The two tones selected for the short interval were between B and C, the second and third tones where A is the fundamental, and E and F, the fifth and sixth tones. Hence, there are no B or E sharps and no C or F flats. If all this sounds like a design of madness, remember that it was done in desperation. The physics of the vibrating string produced an interval too small to be distinguished and recalled. Simple division of that scale produced a series of steps with an innate dullness, but this demonstrated that something as simple as a musical scale can have an emotional effect.

The act of picking 7 of the 12 tones from the chromatic scale (the eighth tone is the first harmonic) left 5 tones and a set of choices for other systems within the basic scheme. These alternatives are called the *major* and *minor* scales. A major scale is one in which the half tones are between the third and fourth and seventh and eighth tones. A minor scale is one in which the half tones are between the second and third and fifth and sixth tones. The best way to study musical scales is against the standard of frequency in cycles per second. In the accompanying illustrations the mid-range tone is A 440 because it is a tuning standard, is easily found on the piano, and is the first harmonic of the fifth string on the guitar. In addition, it is the string from which the guitar is generally tuned, and the 220 cycle fundamental in the illustrations is the sound of the open plucked fifth string. The frequency produced by the guitar at the first fret of the fifth string is 238 cycles per second, at the second fret 257 cycles per second, and so on up to 440 cycles at the twelfth fret.

One of the most popular scales in composition is the C-major scale, and you will note that it contains no sharps or flats. This makes notation and reading relatively simple, and it simplifies playing some instruments, particularly the keyboards because there it is played all on white keys. If you play up and down this scale for a few minutes, you will find that certain melodies come to mind either from recollection or invention. That is the nature of the western musical scale; it says something to you when you play it. Compare the experience of the C-major scale with that of the F-minor scale. The F-minor scale is a scale with four flats and an internal progression that suggests other things. If playing up and down this scale a few times doesn't begin to do anything to you, try playing the first five notes, then repeat the pattern, and then hit the sixth tone. What follows, the playing of the fifth, fourth, third, and back to the fourth tone, is about as natural an impulse as a person can have. This is the act of musical composition, a very normal process within the defined limits of a scale. The outstanding importance of the scales is that they invite the creative impulse.

The relationship between scales and keys is very simple. A melody in the key of F minor uses only the notes of the F-minor scale. Similarly, an F-minor chord may include only the notes of the F-minor scale. Note that in the illustrations of the major and minor scales the bottom note is the fundamental. This tone is referred to as number 1, and we count upwards in the direction of the octave, or first harmonic. A *major tonic chord* uses tones 1, 3, and 5, a *dominant chord* uses tones 2, 5, and 7, a *subdominant chord* uses tones 4, 6, and 8, and the *relative minor chord* uses tones 1, 3, and 6. On some instruments, particularly on the piano, certain tones are doubled, coming from an extension of the scale into the next octave. When that is the case, tones 1 and 5 may be doubled, but 3 may not, and 5 may be omitted, but 3 may not. An understanding of chords can be important in handling many sounds as music because most mechanical devices produce a fundamental tone. Recordings of automobile exhausts, particularly from sports cars, will show a detectable fundamental. You can find it by playing the recording while you strike tones on a xylophone, guitar, or piano. Suppose that the car in the opening sequence described in the beginning of this chapter had a fundamental of G. According to the rules, a garbage-can lid with a natural frequency of B or D could be used to produce a melodic sequence, or one

144

C/S	A	B	C	D	E	F	G
880							
843							
806							G'
769							F♯
733						F'	
696					E'	E	E
660					D♯		
623				D'		D	D
586				C♯	C♯		
550			C'			C	C
513		B'	B	B	B		B
478		A♯				B♭	
440	A'		A	A	A	A	A
422	G♯	G♯			G♯		
403			G	G		G	G
385	F♯	F♯		F♯	F♯		
367			F			F	
348	E	E	E	E	E		
330		D♯					
312	D		D	D			
293	C♯	C♯					
275			C				
257	B	B					
238							
220	A						
			AM	BM		DM	EM

C/S	A	B	C	D	E	F	G
880							
843							
806							G'
769							
733						F'	F
696					E'		
660						E$\flat$	E$\flat$
623				D'	D		D
586						D$\flat$	
550			C'	C	C	C	C
513		B'			B		
478			B$\flat$	B$\flat$		B$\flat$	B$\flat$
440	A'	A		A	A		A
422			A$\flat$			A$\flat$	
403	G	G	G	G	G	G	G
385		F$\sharp$			F$\sharp$		
367	F		F	F		F	
348	E	E		E	E		
330			E$\flat$				
312	D	D	D	D			
293		C$\sharp$					
275	C		C				
257	B	B					
238							
220	A						
	Cm	**Dm**		**Fm**	**Gm**		

146

with a frequency of G# could be used to generate dissonance. The effect of having two sounds of this kind within one-half tone of each other is absolutely grating. The relationships within music are fairly simple, but often it seems that there are many of them.

In addition, there are many different types of musical instruments. However, an important system of classifying and understanding them in terms of the tones they produce can be developed. It is perhaps fitting to start with the plucked stringed instruments. If we could see tones in a two-dimensional system wherein the flow of time proceeds on the horizontal axis and the disturbance of air molecules proceeds on the vertical axis, the plucked string tone would appear as follows:

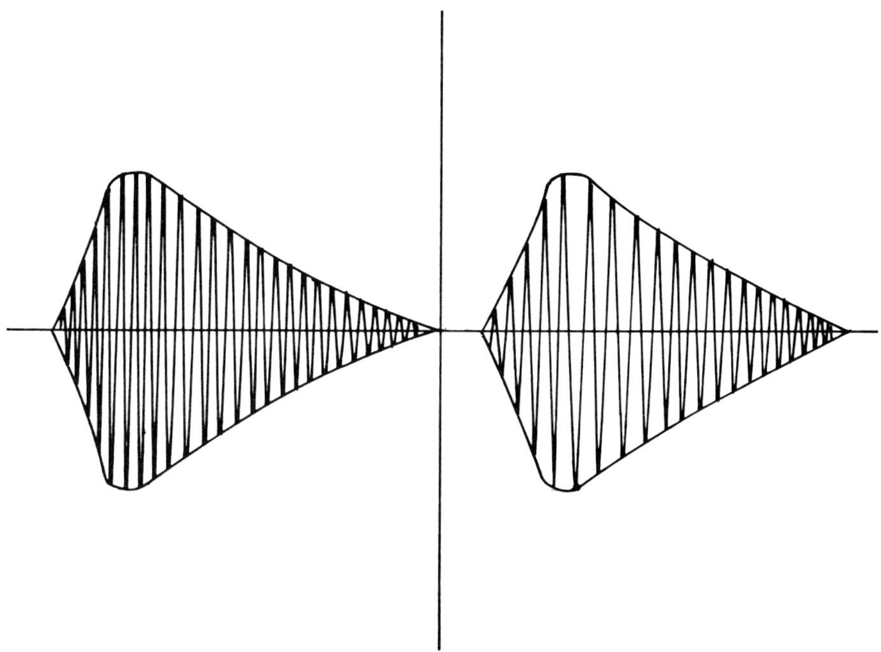

Note that the intersection of the vertical and horizontal axes is what is heard *now.* We have heard one tone and soon will hear another. The note's attack is sharp, virtually instantaneous, as it rises to the maximum disturbance of the air. But there is no duration in these notes; the decay sets in immediately and is rapid. The production of the second tone is distinct with no portamento, or sliding, between tones.

All bowed instruments, violin, cello, and so forth, produce this type of tonal pattern:

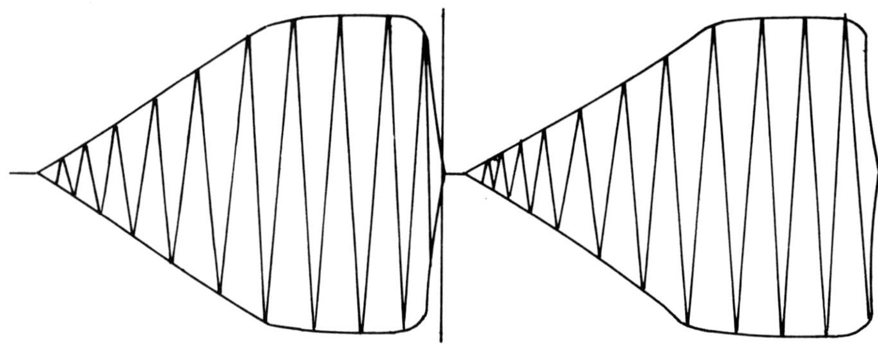

The attack is long, the duration (a function of bowing) is long, and there is no decay in normal playing. Portamento is possible and is something of a problem for beginning players and those who have to listen to them as they search the fingerboard for the correct notes. Wind instruments also have long attacks, long duration, and no decay. The tone ends instantly when the blowing stops. However, wind instruments can also be *tongued,* chopping the air into short bursts by sticking your tongue into the mouthpiece. This technique, illustrated below, gives the wind instrument a sharp attack and a slightly extended decay pattern as the burst of air makes its way through the tubes.

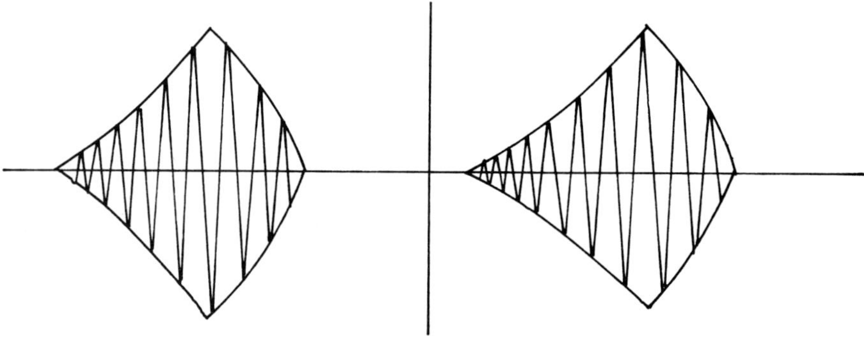

There are many other instruments, but they all produce tones in these few patterns, featuring variations in attack, duration, and decay. There is only one other kind of modulation which occurs in musical instruments, and that is vibrato.

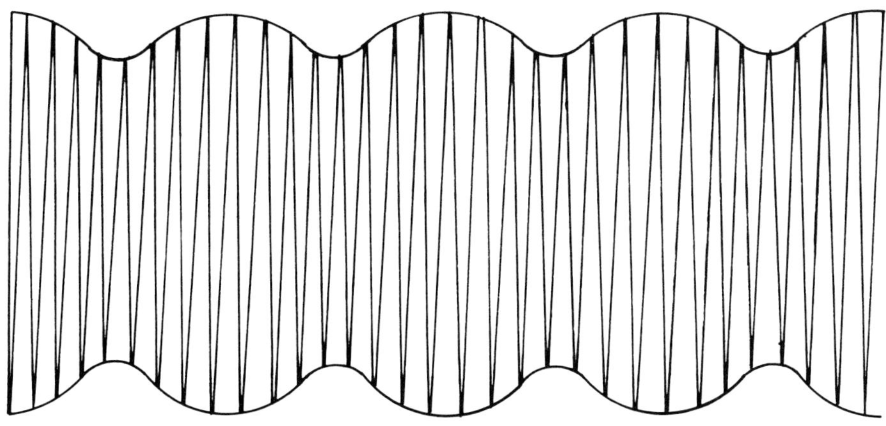

Vibrato is a wavering of the basic tone accomplished in fretted instruments by varying the tension of the finger at the fret. In unfretted, stringed instruments the stopping finger is only moved back and forth. But in wind instruments vibrato usually can be accomplished only by varying the air flow through the mouthpiece. Generating vibrato in some instruments is very difficult and in others, the piano for example, impossible. Just as every musical scale suggests certain use, so does every instrument because of its characteristics. However, there are some new instruments that are becoming very popular for which there seem to be no limits. These are the synthesizers.

SYNTHESIZERS

Synthesizers are electronic instruments which, if properly made, can generate tones with any set of characteristics the player wants. Within the general classification there are two important groups—the keyboard and the programmable machines. In the latter category there is only one unit presently being made, and that is the Buchla. Since the Buchla is a component system, in a typical setup the synthesizer contains a power source, several signal generators, a timing pulse generator, a gate, and a sequencer. This last unit takes the place of the keyboard and actually plays the machine. Each impulse from the timing pulse generator advances the sequencer one step through its eight ranks of controls. Each rank contains three separate channels that can be varied to control tone, modulation, or time. Thus, an eight-tone, or chord, melody line can be programmed on the sequencer. But after it is played, the machine returns to the starting point and plays it again, and again, and again. Hence, the Buchla can become very boring very fast, and the device is best used for generating sound effects, random noise, and other accompaniments. The Buchla program can be

The author at work at his own synthesizer recorder setup. It features a Buchla, Steiner Parker, two sources, and one mastering recorder, as well as Dolby noise-reduction circuitry.

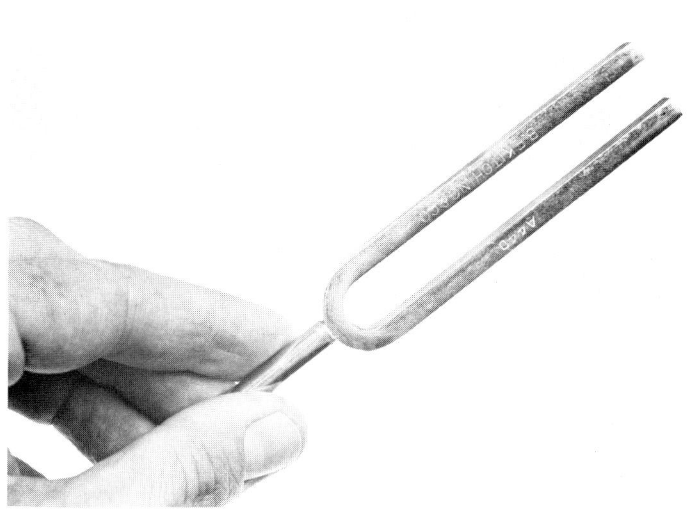

A tuning fork is a simple, but effective, frequency standard on which the musical organization of sound tracks can be based. Synthesizers normally have no base other than the one imposed on them.

varied while it is in progress, but the signal generator and sequencer controls have a range of from 5 cycles per second to 20,000 cycles per second, over 10 octaves, in something less than a single turn of a knob that is either 1.25 or 2.5 cm (½ or 1 in.) in diameter. Thus, it is impossible to play a scale or tune with one of these controls. Nonetheless, these "horseback" variations in tuning and modulation can add much interest to the effect of the machine as long as you don't try to play a melody line.

The keyboard synthesizers are true musical instruments, with the typical machine having three octaves on the keyboard and a control that will extend the range another three octaves in either direction. The typical nine-octave range totally covers the human ear's ability to hear, and thus, the synthesizer is unlimited in this respect. The single limitation most keyboard synthesizers have is that of being able to play only one tone at a time. This means that chords cannot be played. However, the music produced by the machine doesn't seem to suffer all that much. New machines that will play chords are being developed. A few are on the market, but they are very

.Sound Arts is a leading electronic music and sound effects production studio
in Hollywood. Many feature films and television shows have been scored in
this facility.

Jim Cypherd, Dan Wyman, and Bob Walter of Sound Arts. Complicated as
this electronic array may appear to be, its product is meant to be music and
must be organized according to rules.

expensive. The reason for the high price is obvious when you know that the synthesizer has to have a separate oscillator for each tone produced, and usually the oscillators are not used singly, but are used in a chain of two or three where the second and third are used for modulation. Thus, a fully modulated synthesizer capable of playing a three-note chord would have to have nine oscillators, and all would have to be of very high quality because any signal drift would cause distracting effects.

Purchasing a synthesizer can be extremely difficult because few people know enough about the disciplines of electronics and music to know what is needed. Fortunately, most of the brand-name synthesizers are excellent, and there is a single characteristic you can look for that will separate the good ones from the bad ones. A fully usable synthesizer must have a pure *sine-wave generator*. If a sine wave could be seen in the system used to illustrate the tones of the standard instruments, it would appear as follows:

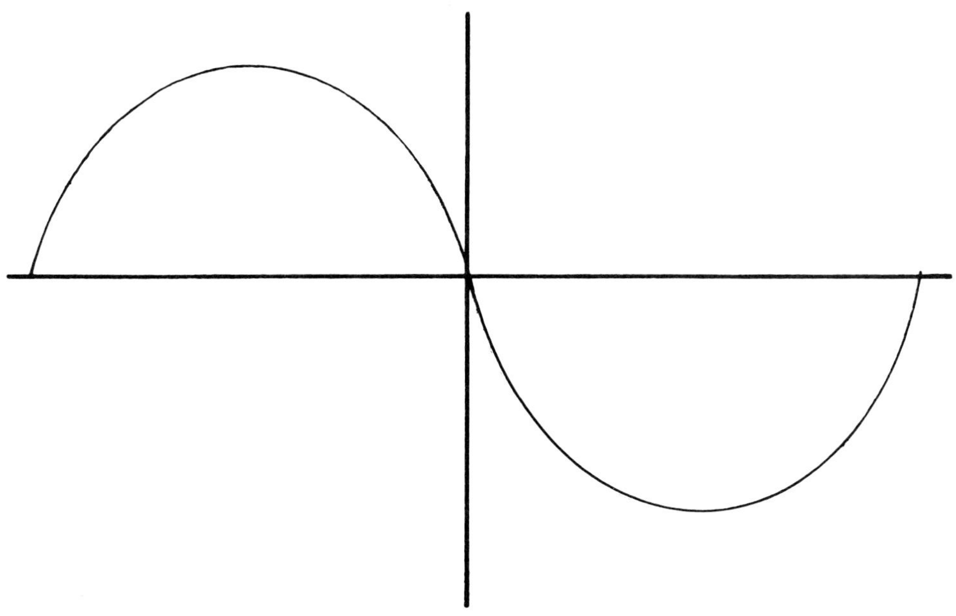

This is a wave form of a fine bell, and it has a ringing tone that is unmistakable. Electronic production of this tone is difficult and expensive, but it can be done and should be a minimum standard for synthesizer purchase. Any deviation from this ideal pattern, as from a saw-tooth or square-wave oscillator, gives the tone a raspy sound that is mechanical and grating. A synthesizer that cannot produce a pure sine wave will sound like a duck trying to sing, and for this reason many of the first machines on the market gave the entire industry a bad name. It would not be fair to identify these machines by brand name because the manufacturers, in some cases, have solved the problem and will solve it in others, and new machines are coming on the market that may have the difficulty in an attempt to shave the price.

With the aid of the keyboard pattern illustrated and a song book (guitar music or piano method book), you should be able to pick out simple melodies on a keyboard synthesizer. It does take some practice, but the pattern soon becomes internalized, much like driving a car, and soon you'll be playing like a pro. Normally, the A on the left side of this pattern will be A 440, and the A on the right will have a frequency of 880 cycles per second. When the instrument is in its mid-range setting, this section of the keyboard will be on the far right of the instrument. There may be an additional C key to the right of the illustrated B, but if you look for the black-key pattern of 3-2-3, you can become oriented quickly. The black keys are the half-tones, or sharps and flats. As noted earlier, in the current system there are no B and E sharps nor C and F flats.

When you first begin to play with synthesizers, there is a great temptation to make them sound like traditional instruments or something from outer space. To satisfy the first urge many of the electronic instruments come with preset stops, which may be labeled flute, oboe, and so forth. Unfortunately, many of these electronic imitations only sound like poor substitutes, giving your track a cheap sound. In most situations the synthesizer works best if it is used in a straightforward fashion, generating a sound that cannot be produced by an ordinary instrument. Even the very "spacey" sounds that can be produced with these instruments can be handled musically and have to be, or they will distract from the content of your production.

To illustrate this case let's take the situation in which you want to generate the mystery of a distant oboe, but you want it to fade into the crash of a pounding surf at sunset. Traditionally, you would record an oboe theme, ideally original but more likely an adaptation of some public-domain music, and fade up the surf sound as the oboe fades down. In this case the oboe is

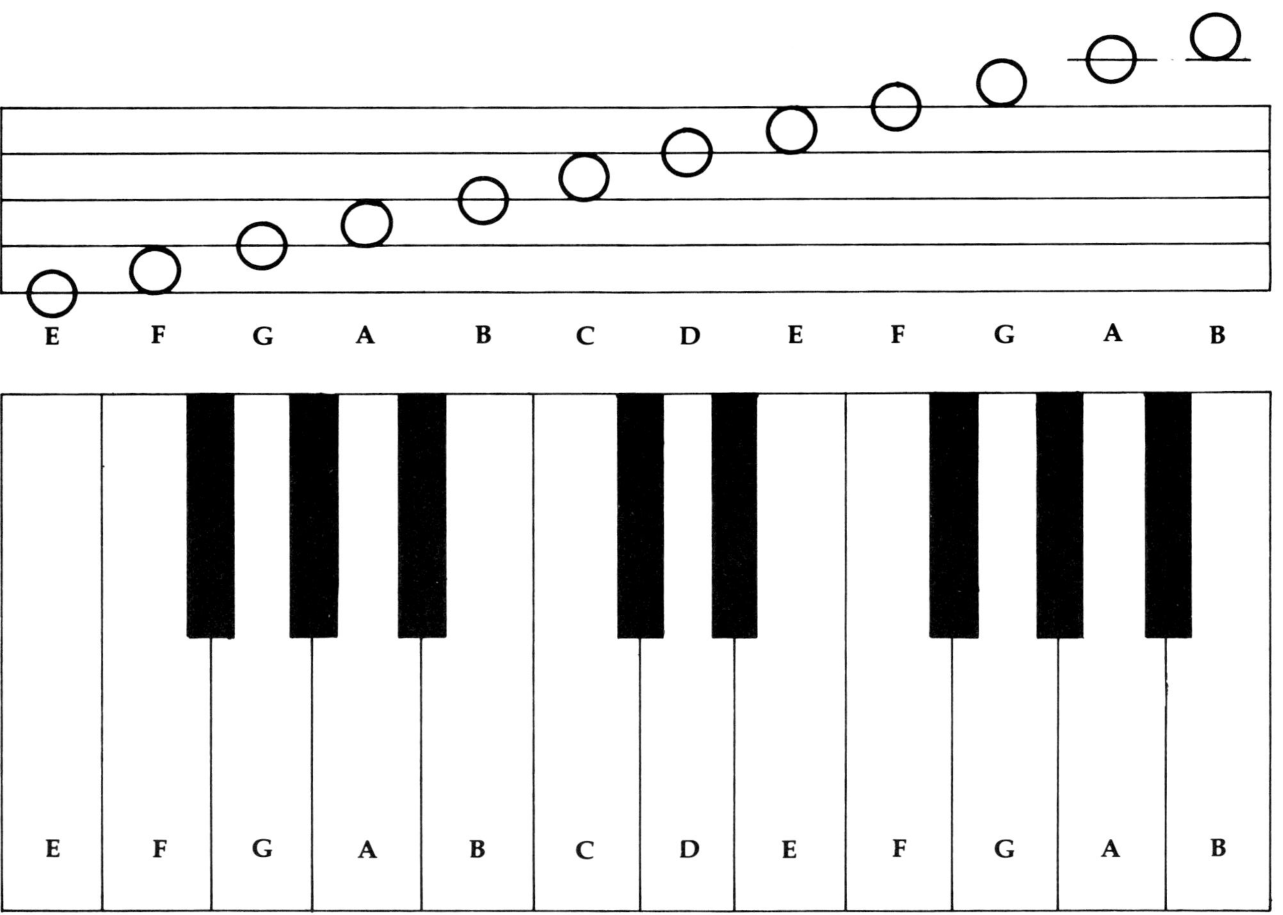

E F G A B C D E F G A B
E F G A B C D E F G A B

never part of the surf sound; it simply melts into it. If this problem is approached with a synthesizer, the result is very different, if preferred. First adjust the machine to produce the sound of the traditional oboe. The oboe produces a raspy tone because the oscillator element within it is a split reed. This tone producer climbs to its maximum amplitude, or air displacement, very quickly and decays with equal rapidity to produce a spiked wave form. However, the oboe attack pattern is long and flowing, inasmuch as it is a wind instrument, and the duration and decay patterns are variable according to breath control. It is a simple matter to set this up on the synthesizer and add some reverberation for the effect of distance.

Most synthesizers contain white and pink noise generators. White noise is the sound of static as can be heard on a radio between stations, and pink noise is modulated with a tone, giving it a more ordered sound rather like that of a surf. As the melody is played, the level of the pink noise can be raised and coupled to the keyboard so that the striking of each note produces another wave. Some synthesizers have a second "envelope" generator; the envelope is the shape of the attack, duration, and decay. This can be hooked up to the pink noise generator to produce the shape of the crashing wave you want to make. The total effect is that of music playing nature, where the sound of the oboe is totally in tune with the surf. The fading sound of the oboe is not a melting of the instrument into a background as much as it is a marriage with it. Once we have set this pattern, we can return to the surf and call our instrument from it logically and cleanly within the framework of the program.

COMMERICAL MUSIC AND SOUND LIBRARIES

Thus far we have been talking about creating our own music and effects. However, often this is not practical nor the most economical alternative. There are several commercial libraries of music and sound produced for audiovisual production. Perhaps the best known and most available of these libraries is the one owned by the Capitol Record Company. This library, which is continually being updated and revised, includes music primarily, but the instrumentation is infinitely varied, and the design of the compositions is purely audiovisual. They have absolutely every kind of little intro and close you can imagine, themes that sound mechanical, poetic, quiet, active, and so forth. Furthermore, if you go to one of the Capitol offices or to a large studio that has the library, you can usually say, "I want an intro and close that suggest the sound of nature existing in quiet harmony." The

Ole Georg is the National Director for Capital Production Music, a division of Capital Records. Well known for his ability to pick correct musical cues, Georg is also responsible for the production of much of this extensive library.

person in charge will look thoughtful for about 3 seconds and say, "Let's try 381, cut seven." When the record or tape is played, 90 percent of the time it will be exactly right. Of course, these people live with this music, and if you are in the Hollywood office in the Capitol Tower, you are dealing with some of the people who make the music, and they are really tuned to it.

One of the drawbacks of the Capitol library is that it is so good it has been used to death. This is the reason that they are continually revising it. However, it is hard for them to stay ahead of the producers, and in this business, just as in popular music, certain themes become hits and suddenly

Ole Georg displays a new release in the Capital Production Music offering Media Music. *This library is especially adapted to audiovisual production.*

everyone is using them. A friend of mine in Hollywood had this kind of thing happen to him one time too many, and he decided that in his next filmstrip series he was going to have original music. He convinced the publisher that the investment would be worthwhile and launched into a great fiasco, working with a composer and musicians. When he finished, we were all amazed at how much his sound tracks sounded like Capitol's music and for about 10 times the cost! Certainly, there is a place in the audiovisual business for original music, but the production of it is not without hazard. The one place where original music really pays off is in a large film or filmstrip project in which one of the specifications is wall-to-wall music. Most audiovisual producers use instrumental introductions and closes but leave much of the program track open for sound effects, narration, dramatic readings, and an occasional musical accent. None of the existing music libraries are designed for wall-to-wall, and the relatively short cuts either become distracting or repetitive. Also, the longer classical pieces cannot be adapted to films or filmstrips without completely taking over the entire show. Good classical music is just too attractive, and the bad music is something you don't want anyway. Original music for audiovisual productions is a very special kind of music, timed and very much in tune with the story. The more ordinary audiovisual program will include sound effects only in the body of the program.

RECORDING SOUND EFFECTS

The area of sound effects illustrates another odd fact about the audiovisual business, that is, the real thing seldom sounds like it. In part this is true because most productions are played on inexpensive reproduction systems, and excellent effects that sound great on your studio recorder will fall flat coming through a motion-picture or cassette playback system. It is necessary to transfer your effects to a cassette player to see how they will sound in the final production, and the experience is a revelation. You soon learn that a fully effected and scored sound track can work against itself in all its busy confusion. After the introduction the occasional musical accent is more effective than the constant droning of an unresolved chord sequence. As a general rule, avoid musical resolution in audiovisual scores to prevent an ending in mid program. This can become its own kind of distraction. The narrow response of the cassette player will demonstrate that the sound effects you use will have to be rather direct and the audio equivalent of capital letters without being overly loud. A sound effect that has to be mixed in so intensely that it covers the narration or reading is the wrong sound effect.

Seldom are sounds in nature ever separate or isolated. The background ambience can sometimes be filtered out when the effect is transferred to master tape, but often it cannot. The classic problem is that of handling the sound of a pneumatic jackhammer. This machine produces an entire range of frequencies from high-range "singing" of the bit on concrete to the low-range vibrations of the piston motor. In most cases in which you can record the sound, it comes with the roaring of other machines, construction workers' voices, honking automobile horns, and wind. The three types of filters—high, low, and bandpass—screen high frequencies, low frequencies, or high and low bands of frequencies, altering the sound so much that the machine doesn't sound like a pneumatic hammer. The best solution is to find a case in which a pneumatic hammer is being used in relative isolation and to record it early in the morning because most locations are quieter then. However, if you are stuck with a particular effect, the only way you can plug it into your show is to first fade in a background of construction-site sounds, and when the hammer pops on, the ambience with it will seem to be part of the normal background.

Recording location sound effects is now a simple job, whereas it used to be a major production. There are several small, lightweight recorders using reel-to-reel tape, the Sony 800 B, for example, that are excellent for this work. A high-quality directional microphone, like the Electrovoice RE 15, will give you usable recordings of sound effects, voice, and even location music. Straight sound effects, like the pneumatic hammer, can be recorded with small cassette machines, but the sound should then be transferred to a reel-to-reel tape for editing and mixing work. At the time of transfer you can do any filtering needed, and then the stored effect will be ready for any use. Most tunable synthesizers, like the Steiner-Parker, higher quality Moogs, and Arps, contain filter panels through which you can route your sound for cleaning. I mention this specifically because the smallest of the mixing and filtering units available costs nearly as much as a synthesizer. Thus, another reason for buying one of these instruments.

Filtration can help sound effects considerably, but anything you can do at the time of recording to isolate and focus the sound will have a greater net effect per unit effort. The Electrovoice RE 15, probably the most frequently used microphone in the field, is quite directional but can be further focused with the aid of a simple tube of paper rolled so the head of the microphone slides into it. The length of the tube controls the degree of focus, and the tube should probably be no less than 5.1 cm (2 in.) in length nor more than 20.3 cm (8 in.) long. There is one effect that you have to be on your guard for, and that is the natural resonance of the tube, or the "organ pipe" effect. All tubes, either closed or open on both ends, have a natural frequency of vibration, and if you should be so unlucky as to cut a length of tube that is in tune with the fundamental of the machine you are recording or even the natural frequency of the room in which you are recording, the sound on your tape will be unusable. An odd phenomenon like this requires that you monitor your machine while recording. If a resonance is occurring in the system, the earphone will tell you because it is reporting what the system is putting on tape.

One of the more interesting resonance problems that I've had occurred when I was doing the sound effects for my filmstrip series "The Metric System" for Universal Education and Visual Arts. The effect was to accompany a scene taking place in antiquity. While an early philosopher works at his star chart, we are told how the concepts of the year and the 360-degree circle evolved. I wanted to hear the sound of distant gongs reverberating and changing along a minor melody line. I used a small xylophone recorded at 7½ in. per second. When played back at 15/16 in. per second, a speed reduction of eight times, the little bells had the sound of great gongs as they dropped three octaves. The first test worked quite well, but I wanted to focus the response of the microphone so that I could be at a certain distance at the moment they were struck and move toward them as they began to fade, undamping their response. This would give them a true large-gong characteristic.

To focus the microphone I made a paper tube about 10.2 cm (4 in.) long and taped it to the microphone head. The system appeared to be perfect until I hit the note G, at which point the recorder's VU meter went off the scale, and my earphone reported severe distortion. The resonant length of the tube was right on G, and changing to another length probably would not have helped the situation much because I was playing the full scale. The simplest solution, especially since the tube had been working so well, would have been to compose a melody with everything but G's. However, I elected another course. Cutting a few small holes in the base of the tube near the point where it met the microphone destroyed its ability to resonate strongly within my working range and still left the level of performance high enough to be workable. In this isolated recording situation I could make this modification because I did not want to screen sounds from the side of the microphone. Usually, you won't have to make modifications of this kind, since a simple change of length will get the tube off the resonant frequency.

There are special-purpose microphones for every recording situation, and one of the more popular ones now seen on motion-picture and television sets or locations is the condenser *shotgun*. This very sensitive unit will isolate voices so well that it has eliminated much of the dubbing work that used to have to be done after a location shot. All professional motion pictures are made in what is called a double system, wherein the picture and sound are recorded into separate mechanical systems—camera and tape recorder. The existing single-system units, which have a stripe of tape running down the side of the film, are of such low performance that they cannot be used, and most productions require a mixed sound track anyway. In double systems the camera and recorder are linked electronically by a sync pulse which is generated by the camera and recorded on a separate track of the tape. The timing impulse is then used to synchronize picture and sound when the film is edited. In recent years the world has become so noisy with automobiles, trucks, and aircraft that most motion-picture sound tracks have to be made by rerecording the actor's lines, timing them with the tape made on location, and then mixing them into the final sound track. This is a very expensive process in terms of time and money, and the very narrow response pattern of the shotgun microphone has helped to eliminate much of this reworking.

Special-purpose microphones can help to isolate sounds and make them usable, but what do you do when a properly recorded sound doesn't have the proper effect? A typical example of this is a wind effect. I have never heard a wind recording that sounded like the genuine article. Every sound man in the business has his own system for generating a wind effect, and now much of it is done with synthesizers, using the white and pink noise generators. Recording sounds and playing them backwards or at different speeds can make them more effective or even unique. I once went to some trouble to record the sound of a computer printer, and on playback it sounded like a poor typist at work. You have to judge very quickly whether or not a sound is going to work because listening to it for any length of time permits you to become adjusted to it and project into it whatever is needed. But, the first time I heard the sound of the computer printer at work, I got a flash of a child trying to type. The solution to this problem was to record an IBM Selectric typewriter at 9.6 cm. (3¾ inches) per second, while I pecked at an occasional key. I also had "snooted" the microphone with a 15.2 cm (6 in.) long paper tube and carefully aimed it around the interior, picking up the sound of the motor, gear and chain trains, clutches, and dogs grinding away at the flying ball. On playback, the sound of a frantic machine at work, with all its programmed precision, was clear. There was no other image you could associate with that sound, and it was as genuine as a plastic pear.

CREATING SOUND EFFECTS

The making of sound effects is the subject of several books, numerous articles, and the guarded notebooks of many a sound man. The careful crumbling of cellophane makes a great fire sound, but I prefer to burn some leaves in an outdoor barbeque because you get the snaps and pops of a fire

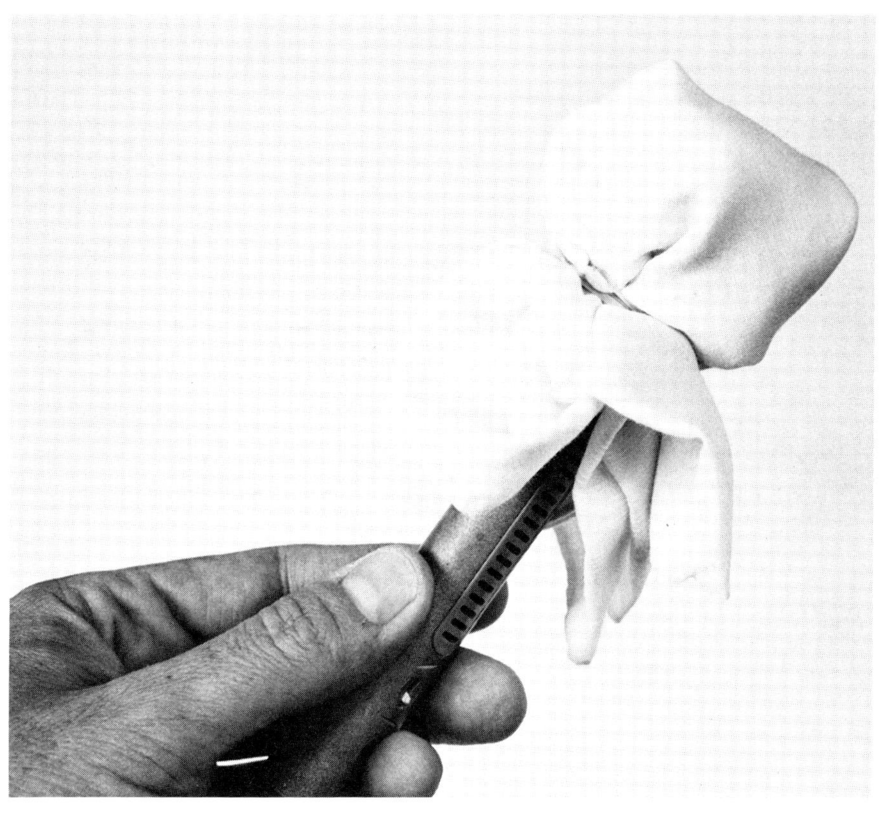

A simple and effective "wind sock" is a folded handkerchief used with a rubber band. It eliminates wind sounds in location recordings.

with too much air. Cellophane doesn't pop authentically. A large coffee can with lid can make a great tumbling container for gravel, marbles, and nuts and bolts for making the sound of a landslide, earthquake, or other cataclysm. The original recording has to be slowed to one-half or one-fourth speed for the proper effect, but this is easy with a machine like the Sony 800 B. Footsteps on various surfaces can be recorded while carrying the recorder and dangling the microphone a few centimetres from your feet or the feet of the model. An iron frying pan or pancake griddle heated to a high temperature will make a wide variety of hissing, frying, and small explosion sounds when small amounts of water are dropped onto it. The microphone has to be held quite close to the spurting droplet, but not so close that it will get wet. The recorded sounds can be played at various speeds for any of several effects. Opening and closing doors makes curiously distinctive recordings that suggest certain uses. Some friends who do sound effects for the motion-picture business had the assignment to effect a flying-saucer landing; and of course they did most of it on a synthesizer with overlapping tracks of hissing jets, "laser" shots, and everything weird you could imagine. At the moment when the hatch was supposed to open, they needed a particularly mechanical, heavy-duty effect. They recorded many car doors being opened, but didn't find anything even nearly right until they came to a 1972 Buick Riveria. Somehow this latching system sounds as if it comes from outer space.

There is one new area of sound-effects production that a few workers are finding very exciting, but others are discussing in hushed tones or heated arguments. Subliminal inputs, which were used effectively in the motion picture *Jaws* in the form of single still frames of the shark's mouth attacking the audience, are possible in sound tracks by either stretching or compressing words so they cannot be recognized consciously. According to the subliminal perception theory the words will be perceived by the listener and contribute to the forming of an attitude. Advertising people are most excited about this new field and are supposed to have used it effectively for several decades. "Buy" and "sex" are two subliminal inputs that can be handled easily and are supposed to be effective. Beyond these fairly simple and obvious messages the subliminal mode becomes complicated, and it is hard to anticipate whether or not its use will be effective. This area of sound production is so new that there are as yet no rules, and everything attempted in it should be thoroughly audience tested. In addition, the mechanical difficulty of getting a usable reproduction at the consumer end of the line may ruin much subliminal sound work.

RECORDING THE NARRATION

By far, the most important consideration in putting together an audiovisual sound track is that of the narrator or actors and actresses. Generally, it is just not possible to obtain acceptable performances with nonprofessional people. Also, the act of committing yourself to nonpro talent, because they seem to speak so well off camera or microphone, can cause great embarrassment when you have to redo their work with a professional voice and at double the studio expense. The fact that someone has worked as an actor, actress, or narrator is not always sufficient in itself. My first narrator was a friend who had been a broadway actor, had co-starred in several major motion pictures, and had his own television show for one season. However, at the time I knew him he was doing character parts or an occasional lead in a stock-car racing picture or the like. Our one attempt at his doing educational film narration was a disaster. The subject matter was science, and in spite of a rehearsal that seemed to go fairly well, in the recording session he fumbled one word after another and ranted and raved at the script, which I had written. To make matters worse, the day was rather hot, and the studio's air conditioning was virtually ineffective. By the end of what should have been a one-hour session, but which took four hours, he was all but naked, wearing only a sodden tee shirt. By the time we left the place, I felt as if I had lived my entire life in a single afternoon.

Mistakes of this kind can be avoided with a simple test. Take a single page of your script and make an appointment for the test at some time convenient for the studio. They probably won't charge you for it because you are going to have them do the actual recording. In the few minutes it takes to read a single page a few times, or even to read a few pages, you will know whether or not the person can cut it. A real pro narrator sits down with the script, reads it virtually cold from top to bottom, and does not make a single mistake. He or she may want to retake certain sections of it for different inflections, but in the main the thing will be usable. If you have to pay union fees, approximately $100 per filmstrip or single 16 mm reel, which is 10 to 12 minutes in either case, the person is being well paid, and you shouldn't have to put up with any problems. Furthermore, if your client is in a position in which he or she cannot be bothered by unions, you should not have to pay such high fees. Generally, if you price a job so the narrator is getting about $100 per hour and knows that he or she will be paid at the end of the session, you will have no trouble getting narrators. This is only one-fourth the regular fee, but it is considered equitable by many actors and actresses. In addition, there is something fundamentally wrong when a union actor can be hired for a full five-day week for less than $500 but must receive almost exactly the same amount of money for reading an hour of narration.

I have never been afraid to compliment actors and actresses, or anyone, for that matter, who was working for me. Some producers are afraid that actors, actresses, and models will want more money if they get the idea that you think they're good. Not true, as long as they don't get the idea that they're indispensable. It is quite one thing to say to talent, "I really like your work!" It is quite another to say, "Where have you been and how could I ever get along without you?" The first statement can be and should be true, and the second is obviously false. Also, I've made it a policy, since my first mistake, never to make friends out of talent. A professional relationship between writer-producer-director, or any combination thereof, is one that needs a little space.

If you are a beginning director or working with a new narrator, you must rehearse. I like to give my scripts to the actors and actresses a few days before the session. Bear in mind that most of my productions are rather short and memorization is not required. If you are doing something on the order of a half-hour show and memorization is required, the actors and actresses will have to have the final scripts for at least a week and better two, but not too far in advance or they'll let it slide. Most professional narrators will study a script for word pronunciation, make pencil notations for inflection, and generally will mark those aspects important to the delivery on their copy of the original. A rehearsal session is extremely important with a new narrator, as here you will find out what he or she cannot do or say. As I mentioned before one of my favorite narrators cannot pronounce the word vague. In spite of his otherwise flawless delivery of everything else in the language, this word throws him. In a case such as this, there is no choice but to change the script, and it is much more convenient to do it in the informal setting of a rehearsal than in the pressed confines of a recording studio while the hourly charges mount.

I prefer morning recording sessions because I am a morning person, but I have found that most people in music and acting businesses are not. Thus, I have learned to set up sessions in the afternoon or at least not to schedule them before 10 AM. It is also a good idea not to schedule a recording session for Monday morning. Recording studios are always cold or stale on the first morning of the week, and the people involved in the session probably will not be at their best. All of the little bits and pieces of machinery, odds and ends of tape, and so forth will be piled here and there from the previous week's work. Recording studios need Monday to get things back in shape, and Tuesday, Wednesday, and Thursday are the best days for recording sessions. Some music recording is done at night, in part because many musicians don't play all that well until the sun goes down, but also because a city is quieter then and there is less trouble with aircraft noise.

A recording session should go very smoothly or something has not been done correctly. The script copies should be absolutely readable, double or triple spaced with any corrections clear. Most narrators will not have trouble with script paper noise, but a single paper "pop" or "crackle" can ruin an entire film or filmstrip narration if you don't catch it and do a retake immediately. It would seem that a mistake is easy to correct; you would simply have to return to the studio, set up everything the same way, record the single line, and cut it into the place where it is needed. But, it doesn't work that way. It is virtually impossible to get everything set up as it was even 24 hours earlier, and voices change from day to day. You cannot drop in so much as a single word without its being apparent that it was recorded at a different time. The one exception to this which I have experienced was in the case in which we had a narration running through some really complicated sound effects. The sequence should never have been written that way because the effectiveness of it depended entirely on the final balance of narration, effects, and music. The narrator's one line through this complicated audio sounded fine at the time of recording, but during the editing and mix it became apparent that it was not as clear as it could have been and was probably going to be lost in mud. The more I played with the various pieces of tape the less I liked it. But rather than call the actor back to the studio for a retake, I decided to do something that would give me a more effective reading in the first place.

I made an appointment to meet the actor at his home. We found a place that would give us a crisp, slightly resonant recording—a room with hard walls as opposed to the studio's super-soft acoustically tiled walls and ceiling. Mixing this take into the conglomeration of effects and music gave me the clarity of track that was needed to carry it. Ironically, I probably would not have wound up with as good a final mix if my man had read this one line of the script as effectively as he had the rest of it. But, when making a master tape you have to be very careful not to let stray noises, such as paper "pops," get into the track in a place from which they cannot be removed. I have found that taping the script pages to thin cardboard stops all of this noise, and whereas this was a practice that I originally used on an occasion when I was working with a fairly nervous actor, I now do it for everything. Any large art supply store carries a material called *railroad board* in a 55.9 × 71.1 cm (22" × 28") size. You can have them cut it into fours on their paper cutter, and it will make four 11" × 14" sheets from each sheet. Tape the top and bottom of each script sheet of the narrator's copy, which for most educational productions should be between 12 and 20 sheets, and you'll never have to cut another "pop" or "crinkle" from a master tape.

During the session it is permissible to let actors and actresses drink water that is at room temperature, but do not let them drink hot coffee or cold soda drinks. Not only will fluids of different temperatures affect the frequency output of their voices, but a stomach full of soda inevitably produces a burp. Worse yet, the anticipation of the alimentary event will cause their voices to tense and weaken, and at some level you, and the audience, will know that the event is coming. You will hear it and cut it out, but the audience will only be frustrated. I cannot imagine a script situation in which you would want this kind of anticipatory modulation.

Sound is the last frontier in the audiovisual business. In spite of its peculiar effectiveness in generating emotional responses, music has remained a mystery, but unnecessarily so. However, all of these things have to be worked with before you can use them effectively. Sound equipment is expensive, but it is becoming very much a part of the standard kit of the audiovisual producer.

13

Final Assembly

The day finally comes when your show is on film, the script has had its final seasoning, and you are ready to put the whole thing together. In the audiovisual production business you are almost always dealing with a set of 35 mm slides at this point. It does not matter whether you are making a slide show, filmstrip, multi-image show, television commerical, or motion picture from slides. The principles of editing are the same. The show has to have a beginning, body, and finish, as well as an objective. These points have long ago been settled in the script, but sometimes it is necessary to review them clearly before the final editing is done. Every project develops a personality. The shape of the project usually fits the mold that has been built for it, but nothing always turns out exactly the way it is planned. Opportunities occur during production, and the set of images and the sound track now have things in them that were not originally planned. The unplanned shape of these elements very much affects the outcome of the product.

Just as important as the evolutionary phenomenon in production is the fact that most producers suffer a depression at the end of a project, and in too many cases it hits just before the end of the cycle and not at a more convenient time. This is the one place where I've always admired the motion-picture people, as they have a long tradition of not letting the director, producer, or writer do the editing. Their budgets are usually big enough to support this degree of specialization, and the tradition has developed through pure necessity.

Part of the necessity is due to the fact that a motion picture must come from a set of takes, which are normally inviolate and cannot be changed, added to, or modified other than through some optical trickery. This is a very different situation from that of the audiovisual business. You can usually go back and shoot one more slide or manufacture a transition image to save a sequence. It is feasible for a noncompromising, perfectionist type of person to survive, and even thrive, in audiovisual production, whereas that same person would soon be flat broke in the motion-picture business. In the movies you cannot go over every budget, reshoot many sequences, and dump buckets of money in the special-effects labs and make a profit. But, in the audiovisual business you cannot always accept what comes out of the cameras the first time. The severe limitations of the media require you to throw everything into it.

The nature of the show dictates who edits it. In most audiovisual productions you, the producer, are usually nominated by the process. If the depression which is normally part of the completion process hits before the final editing starts, it may be wise to take off for a few days and do something else. This is especially true if you *know* there are problems in the show. Don't think that you are running from those problems if you take a break. The difficulties will go on your "back burner," and likely as not, a solution will pop up in a few days.

I have had the good fortune to be able to go skiing, diving, or even to a super hot desert on several of these occasions and have never felt that the break was wasted. There is something about being in the mountains or even lifting off the ground at Los Angeles International Airport that really clears my head. The return has always been an eager one, and I also usually have had a good plan in mind. And, it has been a plan that came about naturally and was not forced or the product of sleepless nights.

THE PROCESS

Your script is the guide in the editing process, and it should contain an opening sequence. The nature of that sequence and its own evolution will depend on where you are going. The first question is: What is the nature of the first content visual? Knowing where you have to be at this crucial point in the show will dictate how you are going to get there. In the sample script on lenses (see Chapter 4), we expedited the process by running through the first sequence without narration to establish the location in ultra-wide-angle view, because many people are not used to seeing in this focal length. In all cases the opening has to establish where you are physically and the emotional content of the situation. The information is then painted on this

Horizontal Editing Studios is one of the more convenient, modern television editing studios in Hollywood. Every image can be given an address on tape, and the cutting can be handled electronically with high precision.

background in the form of narration. In some opening sequences you can present printed matter, headlines, road signs, and the like, but this is not so much information as it is a setting of the mood. The ideal opening sequence usually takes about 30 seconds and richly establishes where you are and the feelings present—nothing else.

If the first content frame visualizes an event taking place in a cold exterior environment, then the opening sequence shots should be from that same environment or one very close to it in every way. The color spectrum should be neutral or bluish and never green or red. Blue is emotionally and physically cold, green suggests life in a functioning form, and red reflects warmth or passion. Neutral colors are not colors at all; they are black and white or a gray that is some mixture of the two. Black is the physical absence of any color, and white is the physical presence of all colors in equal amounts. It is the equal presence of all the color/emotional factors that forms white and the emotionless nature that white represents. This is exactly the same situation as in music; the presence of a few vibrations can be musical or dissonant, and the presence of all such sounds results in what is called "white" noise.

The basic principle in setting up an opening is that you are going somewhere. That place, the first content frame, has certain characteristics, and you are coming to them from the utter neutrality of darkness. To overcome what is going on in the audience and to gain control of the situation you have to give one little bit of information about the three channels with which you will be working (narration, sound effects, and music), adding them up to the sum of the first frame.

THE BODY

Editing the body of most shows is comparatively simple because the content follows the script, which followed the outline. The amount of work that has gone into the script and the outline usually ensures that the show will move forward smoothly, present its material, and get ready for a big finish. The exception to this is the show that is done without a script, as in the case of many documentaries, or entertainment productions that change so rapidly the script is meaningless. These kinds of shows are edited painfully and require much gimmicking to create a smooth flow. There is nothing simple or universally true that can be said about this kind of editing problem, as each one of these rolling problem productions will have its own set of difficulties that will have to be solved as you go along.

If there is one universal truth in the editing of a free-form documentary or entertainment show, it is that the sound track will assume a controlling role and the visual elements will have to fall into place with it. This is probably the case because sound is a medium with more limitations than photography. Generally, only one audio event can be happening at one moment. Certainly, there are narration, sound effects, and music happening simultaneously, but if you determine the levels of these three elements, you will find that the latter two will be 2 or 3 decibels (db), and often more, down the decibel scale from the level of the narration. The db scale is logarithmic; 2 db means 100, or in this case 1/100, and 3 db means 1000 or 1/1000. This is really a vast difference in the levels, and it is rather amazing that any use can be made of this subordinate information. Thus, it is the narration, dialogue, or singing voice that will lead when putting the visual elements together in a show that otherwise has no form.

THE SOUND TRACK

Sound-track construction has become a joy recently because so many excellent multi-track recording systems are now available, and so many more seem to be coming soon. Whereas in the past all the various components of music, sound effects, narration, and whatever were gathered on separate rolls of tape, and several playback decks and one recording deck were worked with to make a mix, the whole operation can now be done with two machines. The tracks are laid separately on a single length of tape, and endless experimentation can take place quite simply because the tracks can be moved back and forth, altered, filtered, and modified in many ways as they are installed on the mixing master. The ideal system for most audiovisual productions can be had in something as simple and inexpensive as the Teac four-track machine. This company also makes a series of excellent accessories for the machine: remote control, line mixing, and echo producing devices. It is possible with this one line alone to assemble a studio that will give professional results for a few thousand dollars. This just has not been possible until recently.

The word "professional" is one that has been overworked in both photography and sound. In both of these fields the person who is doing the work is often no more knowledgeable than the amateurs who do it for fun: The primary difference is that the former person gets paid for it. Professional camera bodies have almost always been painted black because they were to be used in applications where any bright, shiny decoration would cast a reflection. Chrome plating is much more functional in most applications, and most of the real pros whom I know have several camera bodies, and most of them are chrome plated. The outstanding characteristic of professional recording equipment is that the line inputs are of low impedence so that long lines can be used to transfer the rather weak sound-carrying currents efficiently. Now the amateur's home equipment is performing as well as many of the professional units, and because the philosophy of building professional recording equipment has changed so much, there is little difference between the two types of units. Twenty years ago a professional recorder was built to last 30 years or more to justify its high cost. Now, with the rapid changes in equipment and the tax advantage of an accelerated amortization schedule, there is little reason to build anything that will last more than 5 years, or 10 at the very most.

The highest grade of professional recorders, those using 2-inch (51 mm) tape and having 24 track heads, are quite another matter. These are still built to the old-fashioned standard of lasting forever, again to justify their high cost and because they have to be more rugged than the Rock of Gibraltar to transport the tape perfectly. And, *perfectly* is the standard in the music recording business.

Sound tracks in the audiovisual business can be prepared to a somewhat lower standard than perfection. The playback systems for filmstrips and video recordings are notoriously bad, but the playbacks for

Horizontal Editing is a modern, good studio for video editing.

slide shows can be as good as the state of the art where you have a free choice of the tape format. In most cases, slide-show playbacks will be done on the Teac machine at either 7½ or 15 in. (19.1 or 38.1 cm) per second. The difference is not great; 15 in. per second does have a higher frequency response and less wow, flutter, and a few of the other tape problems, but the improvement is hard to hear. The main reason for working at 15 in. per second is that it makes tape editing simpler if you have to chop out single words, odd noises, and so forth. This should never be the result of a professional recording session, but it happens. Still, the building of a sound track is begun with the recording of the narration at 7½ in. per second. This reduces the cost of tape and the amount of material you will be handling and storing. It also matches the speed at which the location recordings have been made and permits splicing them into place for the transfer to the four-track mixing master.

Editing tape is a relatively simple craft. It only requires time and a degree of caution, which most people can learn. The one thing that has to be done is to institute a system in which *every millimetre* of tape is kept somewhere and can be retrieved if a mistake is made. This is done by starting the process with a labeled "feed" reel which contains the first portion of the narration. This is rolled onto a take-up reel labeled "OUT" because the beginning of the tape will contain the starting leader, a level setting reference tone, a recorded slate, and the usual "We're rolling . . . " or "Let's do it . . . " conversation from the control booth. As soon as you get to the first usable bit of narration, the tape is stopped, cut, and a long leader is added to the front of the narration. This is run onto another reel labeled "PROGRAM" or "I." You continue with this reel until the narrator makes a mistake, a paper rustle is heard, or some other audible problem appears on the tape.

Splicing is done with a block that can be obtained at any tape-recorder store, and they are quite simple to use. The one problem in cutting tape is that you cannot see the sound on it and must locate the places to be cut by running the tape back and forth over the "PLAY" head. The play head is usually the last of the heads in the direction of the tape transport. In a typical three-head machine the first head is the erase head, which performs the two functions of eliminating any previous recording by sending an alternating magnetic flux into the passing tape and simultaneously adding a *bias* to the tape, thus making it more ready to accept a new recording in a predictable fashion. *Bias* can be compared to raking bare ground. It introduces a surface characteristic of a known nature rather than relying on whatever Mother Nature has done to the tape. If the bias frequency is high and the amplitude low, the surface is rather smooth like that raked with a fine-toothed implement. If the bias frequency is low and the amplitude high, the magnetically permeable surface will have a characteristic more like that of a surface tended with a deep-pronged tool. Laying a recording on this known surface produces a more predictable result, and rather than having high fluctuations in the output of the bare tape itself, the bias frequency treatment tends to make the process outcome more predictable.

The record head is second in the series of heads, and it produces the recording by sending a modulated magnetic signal into the tape, which can then be read by the play head in the playback mode. It is possible to simultaneously record and listen to the playback in a self-checking method of making a recording. We don't do this because it normally slows the entire process when you and the narrator are a little out of synchronization with each other. However, we have had a few instances in which this technique would have been a good idea. I will only do this in a situation in which it will be impossible to get the narrator to return if anything has gone wrong. But, it is the mark of the professional in the audiovisual business that he *never* sets himself up in this fashion. All work done by true professionals is

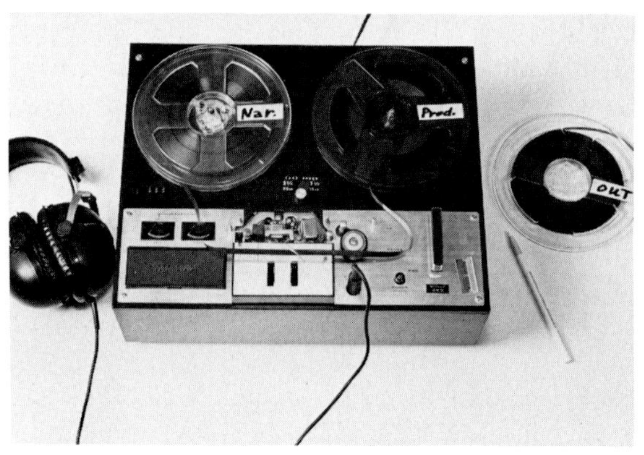

Narration editing
setup with a small
tape deck and earphones.
The PRODUCT and
OUT reels will contain
every millimetre of the
original narration, thereby
preventing costly losses.

Editing block can be
fixed to the top of a location
tape recorder, in this case a
battery-operated Sony
800 B. This will permit
editing in the field, thereby
saving production time.

Editing route
for tape takes it
away from the capstan and
pinch roller. Moving the
tape back and forth by
hand will locate the spots
where the tape can be cut.

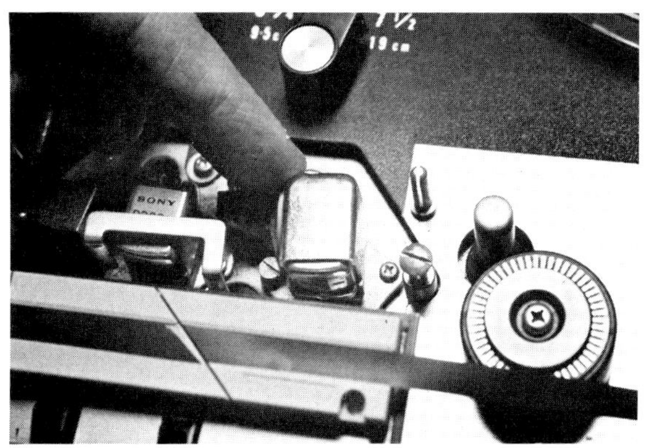

*Playback head
is normally the last
in the series of heads by
which the tape passes on
its way to the take-up reel.*

*A single spot from a
white grease pencil marks
the location for a cut in a
sound track.*

*The tape is then cut with
a single-edged razor blade.
The white grease mark
usually will not interfere
with the splice, but it
may be removed with film
cleaning solvent.*

repeatable, and therein lies its real value.

Marking of those spots where you want to cut the tape can be done with a white grease pencil of the kind that can be obtained at any office supply store. Cuts are made before and after an unwanted paper rustle, other noise, or flub, and the cut portion should be spliced onto the "OUT" reel. If you make it a policy never to throw out a single piece of tape, there will never be a panic caused by loss. Splicing all of these various odds and ends onto a reel may seem like make work, but we have found that it is absolutely necessary and would not consider doing it any other way.

Splices must be made with the special kind of splicing tape made for this work. You won't believe the price for this material, but it is the only kind of tape that can be used for the work. Splicing tape virtually melts into the tape base, loses its edge, and forms a smooth bond in the place where you have cut. Really good splices that have been played a few times and run through the pinch rollers will pass through the machine as smoothly as the tape itself. It is no longer necessary to expect to hear a great clatter, click, and "clink-clop" when a splice passes through a transport mechanism. An experienced editor will hear almost every splice, but it will take trained and experienced ears to pick them out.

In spite of the perfection of the tape-splicing process you cannot use the edited original narration tape for track building. It is still not possible to record in a splice, and the edited narration must be transferred to another generation of tape for the final track building. This is best done going from a full-head narration tape to a quarter track, and all spacing and timing will have to be settled before this transfer is to be made. Ideally, you should anticipate the length of the opening and closing sections, adding enough *room tone* to the back and front section of the narration master to account for these parts of the final sound track. Room tone is blank tape recorded at the time the narration is done, usually at the end of the session, with all control settings the same as those used during the session. This procedure gives a product tape that has all the electronic noise of the system in it—the noise that is normally heard between words and phrases. It is a little more noisy than new recording tape which has had a standard degree of bias added (the electronic "raking" that readies the magnetic surface for the recording), but you can hear the difference if you have to splice in a blank section using raw tape instead of room tone.

Noise-reduction systems, like the Dolby, are becoming a normal part of the recording business, especially in cases in which the product is a cassette. We have not found it necessary to use this equipment in recordings in which the narration is recorded in a studio and the sound effects and music come from good sources. When most of our sound effects are made especially for the shows in which they are used and much of the music is generated on synthesizers in first generation on the mixing master, noise reduction is not needed. But, if you are working with location recordings, canned sound effects, and canned music, the hiss can add up on all these various tracks and really ruin a master recording. In a situation of this kind a Dolby system can be a life saver, and for the few hundred dollars it costs to install it in most mastering setups, the money is well spent. You do have to remember that using a noise-reduction system means that you have to use it from the beginning and on each of the tracks in the sound track, or the final mix with it won't work. Noise-reduction systems encode the sound signal in much the same fashion as a sideband radio transmission, reading the system's noise on the unused side and then electronically subtracting it from the side containing the information and noise. The system really works well when it is handled properly, but it is yet another box to plug into the line and more cables to handle in the ever maddening business of making sound tracks.

When the narration has been recorded on, let's say, channel 1 of a 4-track tape, you are ready to build the entire sound track. In the general plan for doing a filmstrip or information slide show the sound effects are put on channel 2 and the music on channel 3 with cues on channel 4. If we are doing a stereo music show the music will be on channels 1 and 2, the cues on 4, and 3 will often be unused. Any narration will be mixed into the music tracks in the ordinary manner of making a final mix from multiple sources. In all recording of the various tracks, whether it be the narration, sound effects, or music, the recording level should be adjusted to maximum saturation on the VU meter, i.e. 0, regardless of the level at which it will be heard in the final program. The playback levels can be adjusted at the time the final running master or program tape is made. This procedure eliminates what otherwise would be an unacceptable amount of noise from the accessory tracks.

When an effect or music is to be added to a tape, the system must be entered, going into *record* mode, with no signal, or there will be an audible "pop" where the signal hits the tape. This is not to say that all effects must be faded into the tape. In many cases, the effect should pop on and pop off, but it must do this after the track to which the signal is being added is functioning in the record mode. This can be done by editing the effect with paper or plastic leader on either side of the wanted sound. The source machine can then be set into operation and the mastering recorder set up with the tape at no more than a few centimetres from the spot where you want the effect to pop up. When the leader is about to end the effect, hit the playback head of the source machine, start your recorder in the record mode for the correct channel, and the effect will be recorded in the correct fashion. These techniques take a little planning and require some trial-and-error work. The nice thing about building a sound track in this fashion is that you can do it over and over again without destroying anything. In the old method of doing a mix, in which several recorders had to be operated simultaneously or in sequence to make the running master, the process was a nightmare, was expensive, and never resulted in a totally satisfactory product. There was always something that could have been a little better, but the idea of doing it all again was unthinkable. In this multi-track process you can play with an effect until it is either absolutely correct, or until you change your idea and get something acceptable.

Adding the cues in an ordinary information filmstrip or slide show is dictated by the script, but when doing a music show the cues either will be added by beat or according to a time schedule. In programming a multi-image slide show we usually block sections out on light boxes, install the slides in the projectors in the sequence that makes them accessible in the order of the flow of the system, and simply play with the program until the sequence looks right to us. With four people involved in this process the difficulty of having too many cooks is quite real, but when we do get to a point where we are all satisfied, the section usually works amazingly well.

Cueing a show by time used to be a difficult problem for us because our clock is not based on a number system that is in full agreement with our system of counting. Our number system is based on 10; we count from 0 to 9 before we add another digit, as in counting from 1 to 10. But, when counting time we begin counting in base 10 for the seconds, but then switch to another base of 60 to count minutes. And, if enough time is involved, we use still another base of 60 for the number of hours involved. This is really an insane system and one that makes editing according to time almost impossible. Enter the small computer to save the day!

A few years ago we bought a programmable calculator, which is actually a small computer that has a memory and programming functions. Some people will insist that these small machines are not true computers, i.e. they do not have a video display, random access memory, and a few other conveniences. The fact of the matter is that the better of the programmable calculators can do all of the mathematics of the much bigger machines, and that is what computing is all about. But, the important feature for us is that these little machines all contain a clock of a certain kind, and one that typically limits the machine to doing 20 or 30 functions per second. Thus, these machines can be programmed to count seconds, and they will do it in base 10 from here through the next three centuries if they have a 10-digit readout. That should be long enough for any show that ever will be made. A typical program for one of these machines is included in the Appendix.

If we are doing a filmstrip or slide show to music and want certain images to appear at certain moments, the simplest way to go about it is to set up the little computer as a seconds counting clock, start it at the beginning point of the tape, and note each moment where a frame should be changed. In one pass we record all of these numbers as a list on a piece of paper, and in the second we punch the cues into the cue track when the number appears on the face of the "clock". If one of the cues is slightly out of place, it is a simple matter to move it by first spot erasing it on the tape, backing the tape to the previous cue, and dropping in the needed cue in just the right spot.

With this same kind of calculator we solved a similar problem in programming television commercials made from still slides. In a typical case we were to have 30 seconds. In the video "clock" each frame is on the screen

Mounting, sandwiching, and other slide-handling operations are usually best done on or near a flat light box with a glass surface, which will allow cutting and trimming with a mat knife.

for 1/30 second, and there are 30 frames per second. Thus, one of our video commercials contains 900 video frames, and because each slide appearance is an "event," in today's best video parlance, we scheduled each event in advance of getting to the studio. This can be crucially important in terms of dollars spent to do one of these because the typical video commercial producer goes to the studio with a pile of slides, a tape track, and a dim idea. A full quad video system in the best studio will cost $800 per hour, so any wasted time can send the budget out the door. When we go to the studio, the address of each event is down on the script, and we tell the engineer punching the buttons *exactly* where to punch in each frame. As a result of developing this system we do video commercials in one pass, while other producers are fumbling around saying, "Let's try it this way ... "

The ultimate trip for anyone who has fallen in love with this funny century and the word "computer" is found in making a multi-image slide show with one of the computerized programmers that operate power packs for projectors. In a typical setup each power pack will operate three projectors. The entire system typically includes 12 or 15 projectors, but may have close to 100. The programmer can operate anything that can be turned on or off and that will accept an instruction in the form of line current, 110 volt AC, or any manageable voltage. The programming computer is actually a device for controlling currents on many channels. It not only turns them on or off, but it will vary them in a series of steps that ranges from 8 to 32 between *off* and full *on.*

As a general rule, these systems are designed individually, and the full scope of the multi-image potential is a subject far beyond the objectives of this book. I can only outline what the machines can do and cite a few examples of what we have done with them.

THE SINGLE-SCREEN FORMAT

We have used this format very effectively in shows that were to be projected in a room or hotel suite. It usually involves six projectors, because using many more gets cumbersome and keystoning of the images is quite noticeable with more than six projectors on a single screen. This format is quite adaptable to television recording, and since the quality of television imaging is so much lower than film, the transfer works amazingly well.

The six projectors that we normally use in this format can only carry 480 slides, but we have made very successful shows of up to 16 minutes. It may not sound like it, but one slide every 2 seconds, even where many slides

The Image Stream is one of the leading multi-image production facilities in Hollywood. Here, Christopher Korody is programming a sequence for the Diana Ross concert at the Universal Amphitheater.

may be involved in some effects, is really too many. The pace of such a show is relentless and tiring. We have never felt a limitation in working with as few as six projectors and have found that 10-minute shows, which use only half the potential images, seem to be ideal.

The editing of a six-projector show to go on a single screen is very straightforward, differing very little from a filmstrip or straight two- or three-projector dissolve show. Still, you can do some very nice effects with six projectors, popping images all over the screen, and you can do some amazingly believable spin effects. The secret to the spin is to mount the object on a rod with an angular indicator, including markings such that you can rotate the object exactly 30 degrees. The six slides available will give you a full 180 degrees of turn, but when shown it will appear to be a full 360-degree spin because of the two-dimensional nature of the image. If you analyze the appearance of a spinning object in nature, you will discover that you never see more than 180 degrees of motion. But, what you do see is a back side. In some objects the back side is exactly like or very like the front, or you would prefer not to see the back, as in the case of a typical record jacket.

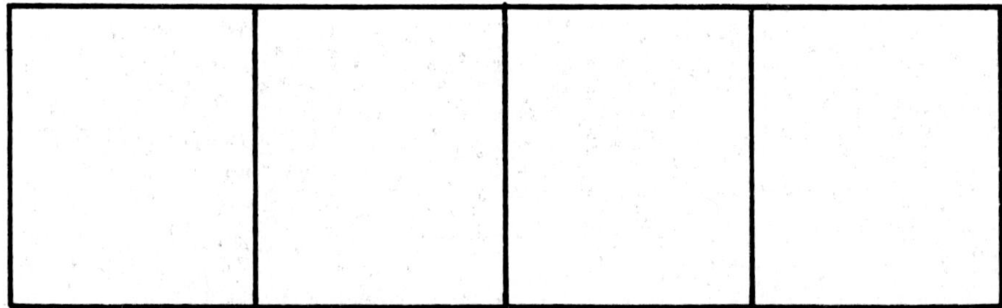

The three-screen, center-overlap format

THE THREE-SCREEN CENTER-OVERLAP FORMAT

This format generally uses 12 or 15 projectors, and it has become a standard for the audiovisual industry because it allows full-screen panoramas and nearly full animation in the center screen area. With so many projectors and a potential of 1200 images you can go to a screenless format much of the time and just burn slides with little images popping all over the wide screen area. When you are editing for this format, it is wise to keep in mind the fact that you are dealing with four half-frame vertical panels, as well as two full fields side by side and the one full field in the center. Most audiovisual producers are not used to thinking in vertical formats, but a lot of source material, posters, book jackets, and buildings are made this way.

THE PANORAMA MASKS

The panorama is achieved by using three projectors in a horizontal line. The image of the first projector on the left incorporates an optical wedge that is clear on the left side and becomes totally black on the right side, graying about one-third of the way across the screen. The middle projector has a wedge that is dead black in the center and faded out to clear on either side, graying to clear on either third of the frame. The right-side field is clear on the right and goes from gray to black on the left. Artwork or a large transparency is copied in a precision camera setup so the panorama is two fields wide with a seam in the center between the left and right frames. However, the center field records this seam area with no line, and because the area in which the seam would be located is blacked out by the masks, the seam is not seen. The selection of subject matter is very important

The panorama masks

in doing one of these effects. The best original pictures or artwork are those which do not contain any straight lines in areas covered by the overlap. A very distinct horizon can be troublesome, and one that is diffused by ranks of distant hills, ground haze, or the mist of a morning sunrise or evening sunset will be far easier and more effective.

THE THREE-SCREEN VERTICAL-SIDES FORMAT

A new format that we discovered recently works extremely well in doing entertainment productions where an act will occupy the center of the stage much of the time. The two vertical panels can actually be cut in two vertically for some very interesting columnar effects with graphics shimmering and flashing on the sides while the act performs in the middle.

The center screen area is elevated about 60 cm (a few feet) to give the projectors clearance, and if the side panels are set up as rotating triangular columns, one side can act as a screen or white surface, one side can be mirrored, and the remaining side can be painted with graphics, the group logo, or whatever. This format can be treated in a screenless manner, with little images popping on and off here and there. A panorama can be generated on the upper portion of the two side screens using the center field, too, if you don't object to the seams. An outer-space star field with flying objects can be made to work very well in this kind of panorama.

It should be clear now that the multi-projector system can be adapted to any situation. There is no hall, auditorium, or dome that cannot be served by some combination of projectors, and any combination of projectors can be controlled by these electronic circuits.

The three-screen, vertical-sides format

In addition to the ordinary projector, which can come on, adjust to any level of illumination, flash on and off, advance, and be turned off, there are channels available to control accessory units that can modify projected images. Some of these accessory units have been used effectively, and a few are waiting for the right opportunity to be used in a show in which they really apply. They include:

1. *The polarizer motiondizer.* Crossed polarizers block light almost totally. A rotating polarizer in front of a projection lens can block light on sections of a slide where polarizing film has been attached to the backing of the film. This material has to be hand cut and glued in place. It is difficult to handle, but in some shows in which mechanical devices need animation to be clearly explained, it is very much worth the trouble.

2. *The kaleidoscope.* To the best of our knowledge this has not yet been used in a multi-image production, but the unit could be made quite simply with two small first-surface mirrors glued into a rotating frame in the manner of the reflecting "V" slit in the child's toy of the same name. The rotating image would look like a flower, and it could be very effective with images of costumed entertainers.

3. *The water mirror effect.* This could be done with a rotating circle of plastic that has been warped in the fashion of the Weegee lens. The degree of warp does not have to be great to achieve the watery reflection effect. Again, to our knowledge this effect has not been used in a multi-image production.

4. *The color organ.* This is a simple electronic circuit that can be attached to any projector and audio amplifier. It varies the lamp intensity in step with the production of certain audio frequencies. Most of these units

work on three channels—low, medium, and high—and they are usually used to operate ordinary line current for lamps aimed at walls, ceilings, and so forth. The color organ has not been used in audiovisual shows to any great degree, but it should see some adaptation in the future, when producers begin to do more with music and straight music shows.

5. *Flashing lights.* The New York Experience is one show that effectively uses electronic strobe lights flashed directly at the audience through the screen and in the auditorium. The effect as used in this case is one of confusion and disorientation, rather like that of the city itself. There are places where these lights can be effective, but if used they must be used sparingly, and they must be of incredible intensity. It is unfortunate that the duration of these units is so short. The light flash is almost over before you realize that it has happened, and often the effect is one of simply lighting the room and washing out the image instead of giving the high-intensity effect alone.

It is possible for these computerized systems to do just about anything to an image, but there is a tendency for the effects to be overused or not used very well. The real hazard in the multi-image business today is that the engineers have total control of the paintbrush, and what we need are more artists who can learn about the mechanical side of the business. This does not mean that a show producer *has* to learn to punch the buttons, but it may help, and it will certainly improve the working situation if the producer knows what can and cannot be done.

The multi-image field is a new medium. It is not a motion picture. It excites, displays, implants, and imprints information in a very different way from real, live experiences or motion-picture representations of them. In some ways it seems that the multi-image systems short circuit reality or movies and take a more direct path to our conceptual centers. There are no moving parts in the brain, and we probably store experiences as still images. It seems doubtful, although we cannot prove it, that we store a motion-picture-type record with a full 30-to-50 frame per second record of our waking past. This figure is cited because it does appear to be the actual visual cycle. In the simplest of experiments we can recall "Mother," "Frank," "John," or "Bob" in our mind's eye, and these seem to come as still images. If those recollections which form ideas are held in this fashion, then we have a ready explanation of the incredible effectiveness of the still-image systems. The fact remains that in tests dating back to the 1940s still-image projection systems were as effective in every case and more effective in some cases when compared to the teaching done by motion pictures.

You can sell the biggest bang for the buck with still-image systems. Filmstrips are made absolutely for the schools, and multi-image shows are perfect for industrial and business clients. These systems are better suited to the needs of their respective buyers than any other present motion-picture system for the price. Still-image systems are often spoken of as *limited* media, and they are in at least one respect. A dramatic story line is best handled by a motion-picture or video process. A still-image presentation of a dramatic story always looks like old news, a recollection rather than now. But, the most severe limitations of these systems have been the producers for them. There is so little integrated talent, so few people who are trained and experienced in several fields simultaneously. We need people who can draw, paint, photograph, edit music and sound effects, as well as do some multi-image programming. These skills are no more difficult to learn than those involved in the motion-picture field, and professional schools and colleges are turning out 10,000 graduates in cinema and television annually. However, no more than 100 will get jobs. Ironically, the multi-image business is just waiting for talent.

There are so many opportunities in the audiovisual business today that it is really hard to believe when you begin to list and add them up. Many will require some selling because the level of general awareness is low. This is almost a mechanically simple selling situation because the fact that the medium works can be demonstrated so easily. Audiovisual media run circles around printed matter in any training program. Critics of our culture claim that this is not a reading generation, but the fact of the matter is that there has never been a reading generation. More books are now being written, published, and read than ever before, but the percentage of people reading them is microscopic. In the audiovisual field we can solve the communication problem. The opportunities are incredible.

Appendix

COMPUTER PROGRAM FOR THE TEXAS INSTRUMENTS "TI 59"
FOR FILMSTRIP/SLIDE SHOW EDITING

Notes:
The standard program loading procedure of "LRN" plus keying the indicated operation is used to install the original program. The program is then recorded on a blank card with the "1," "2nd," "Write" procedure and it can then be recorded in the normal fashion for future use. All exceptions to normal procedure are outlined following the program.

User Designated Keys: A = interval between start of clock, "R/S," and finish. B = interval/number of cues, C = add cue interval to edit cut point. D = start point and E = Finish point

ADDRESS	KEY CODE	KEY	ADDRESS	KEY CODE	KEY
000	42	STO	013	68	NOP
001	01	01	014	68	NOP
002	42	STO	015	68	NOP
003	02	02	016	68	NOP
004	68	NOP	017	68	NOP
005	68	NOP	018	68	NOP
006	68	NOP	019	68	NOP
007	68	NOP	020	85	+
008	68	NOP	021	01	01
009	68	NOP	022	95	
010	68	NOP	023	66	Pause*
011	68	NOP	024	61	GTO
012	68	NOP	025	00	00

ADDRESS	KEY CODE	KEY	ADDRESS	KEY CODE	KEY
026	02	02	051	42	STO
027	76	Lb1*	052	04	04
028	11	A	053	91	R/S
029	43	RCL	054	81	RST
030	02	02	055	76	LBL*
031	75	-	056	13	C
032	43	RCL	057	85	+
033	01	01	058	43	RCL
034	95	=	059	04	04
035	91	R/S	060	95	=
036	81	RST	061	91	R/S
037	76	LBL*	062	81	RST
038	12	B	063	76	LBL*
039	42	STO	064	14	D
040	03	03	065	43	RCL
041	43	RCL	066	01	01
042	02	02	067	91	R/S
043	75	-	068	81	RST
044	43	RCL	069	76	LBL*
045	01	01	070	15	E
046	95	=	071	43	RCL
047	55	÷	072	02	02
048	43	RCL	073	91	R/S
049	03	03	074	81	RST
050	95	=	075	LRN	

In using the program the clock may be started at any point, usually at "0" and it will count seconds flashing each in time. When the program is stopped, by pressing "R/S," *run* or *stop*, the user labeled keys can perform various additional functions: "A" will tell you the interval between the *Start* and *Finish*. "B" will calculate the number of seconds per cue for the interval for a selected number of cues keyed prior to pushing "B." If that sequence is then followed by pushing "D" for the Start point, subsequent pushes on "C" will then give the time address of the previously selected number of events, slides or frames, to fill the time interval. The result is a very smoothly, quickly, and painlessly edited filmstrip or slide show.

INDEX